NOT

What ^ to say to those that are grieving

Pamela Sue Pearson

and

Andrew Allen Smith

Print ISBN: 978-1-7373373-0-0
eBook ISBN: 978-1-7373373-1-7

Library of Congress identifier: Filed In Progress

DEDICATION

To our children still here on earth (Hayden, Hadley, Sarah, Andrew II, Rachel and Kylie) who have stood beside us as we navigate through this journey, the unconditional love you have shared with us, your compassion, your tears, and most importantly the strength you have given us to face each day. I hope you know how important you are to us. To Nat for loving Haley Sue unconditionally, you will forever be a part of our family. To our spouses, Stacy and Dana, who have walked this entire journey with us. To all the family and friends that have been a part of the journey since day one, we cannot thank you enough for walking along side of us, picking us up when we needed it, crying with us, taking our calls no matter what time of the day or night, and encouraging us to take one minute at a time. We will never be able to thank you for all that you did and continue to do for each of us. To all the people who have experienced the depths of grief and the difficult emotions that come with it. To all those who have felt the awkwardness with people who are grieving and those who were unsure of what to say or do when friends or family, acquaintance and neighbors are experiencing grief. Mostly to our Sweet Haley Sue Pearson whose light will forever shine and who has brought so much happiness to everyone she has touched. She will be missed here on earth, now and forever.

The light is always knowledge and knowledge will light our path if we let it.

Contents

Introduction

To start, this book was written with *Love* for all those that were there and are still here to help and support us, pick us up, help carry the burden, cry and grieve with us, each and every day. This book was not intended to point fingers at anyone. We know that *everyone*, no matter what they said or did, had positive intentions as they helped us in the grieving process. They genuinely wanted to help in some way. We know it was all done out of love. We recognize this and appreciate you helping us walk through these uncharted waters. For that we will forever be grateful. Our hope is that this book will help at least one person have a better idea of what helped and comforted us while we were grieving and at the same time know what didn't help us personally. Though we believe that every family is different, and every situation is different, this book is written to help those that are looking for ways to help others that are grieving when you just don't know what to do or say. Unfortunately, when people have to say goodbye to someone they love here on earth, most of the time, words and actions can't change anything. Actually, in most cases people don't know what to say or do and sometimes feel helpless because they can't change the situation. However, people do want to do and say something that will help those that are grieving.

Grief is one of those things that people don't really like to talk about and certainly don't want to personally experience. Walking alongside someone that is grieving is hard to do. It makes us uncomfortable and sometimes even a little awkward. Our hope is as you read through this book you don't think "I have said that before and I feel terrible now". What we do hope is that it just gives you a little insight from someone that has and continues to grieve. We hope this helps you to distinguish what did help us and it might just assist you in the future when someone you know is going through this process called grief. We can't promise it will help everyone. All we know is what *we* experienced. We can share with you what made a difference in our situation in anticipation that it helps you when you are propelled into a situation that most don't want to be in: interacting with those that are grieving. We do know one thing is for certain, everyone is going to die at some point or another, it is 100% guaranteed. Through this book perhaps something we wrote will trigger someone to do something special, say something that just might help someone, or maybe make someone think before they say what they "usually" say when in this situation. Maybe it will assist you in not saying anything at all and just being present for that special someone that you know is grieving. We can make a difference! Just being there will make a difference. What you say can actually comfort those struggling with grief them and sometimes it is what you don't say that is comforting. It might just be your actions that stand out the most to those in the situation.

We can say with much certainty that you could now effectively skip this chapter. You could go on and jump into the meat and potatoes of the book paying attention to list after list of text, fantastic prose, serious summation, and interesting repertoire. This introduction only provides the foundations for the why this book and some of the intriguing stories and not so intriguing stories came to be. It is 100% true that this portion of the book may not give you any great insight in how to help those that are grieving and of course, this particular chapter will not help you if you have just put on a black suit and are rushing to a memorial service.

On the other hand, this introduction may open your mind to some of the facts and ideas that helped us during our darkest days. It may give you a little insight into the authors and the complexities they faced when writing this book. It may open your mind to a series of events that we all wish we could avoid. After all, we are facing the one thing that almost everyone wishes they could avoid: knowing what to do or say when someone is grieving.

We should say now that neither of us are licensed physicians nor psychologists. If you are experiencing unbearable pain or you know someone who is experiencing this type of pain, please seek professional help. A licensed professional can help you navigate through this difficult experience either with therapy or medication. It is up to each individual to determine their needs, but we strongly suggest that those affected seek out some type of professional help along with counseling and spiritual counseling if they are suffering.

We also want to point out that although this book is serious in nature, we are hoping that you receive some of the humor intended to give it a lighter feel. It will not be a boring mess filled with overused quotes from others and endless repetitions that try to numb your mind. Even though we have been forced to take our own journey through grief we understand that many people have run into mental roadblocks that have led to hurt feelings, destroyed relationships, and a disconnect from loved ones. Interaction with someone who is in deep grief does not mean we want this book filled with sorrowful memories or pious poutings. It is our hope that those who contributed to this book and our own experiences will help you remember some things that did and did not help us and many, many things that were extremely important and pivotal in our process.

Let's start with our story. Our family received a call on a cool winter Sunday night in early December. It was a call no parent can or should ever have to receive. It was a moment in time that we will remember where we were and what we were doing, forever. That pain can never be forgotten.

The memories of the next few hours, days, weeks, and months are memories we wish we could erase from the depths of our memory. We wish we could change it. We wish it was a dream. On December 6th, 2020, our sweet 25-year-old daughter and niece, Haley Sue, had been in an accident involving a car and she left earth to go to Heaven for the rest of eternity. We believe without a doubt she is with our Heavenly Father and she is experiencing all the amazing things in Heaven that we will experience ourselves one day. This was and will continue to be the worst day of our lives and something that we will never recover from, while here on earth. Yes, we will have to move forward with life because we have seen throughout this process that life goes on, people go on. No matter how hard you wish time would just stop, it doesn't. Time keeps going, people keep going, life keeps going. We have continued to grieve and mourn every day and we suspect we will do this for the rest of our lives.

The First Night:

I remember calling my brother, who knew that me calling in the middle of the night probably was not to just talk "small talk", unfortunately it was to tell him something no mother should ever have to say. Our daughter, his niece, had been in a fatal accident. As expected, he and my sister-in-law could not gather their things fast enough, find a dog sitter, and get on the road to travel from Michigan to Tennessee. I needed them both, we needed them both.

Upon arrival, the shock had set in and they knew they would be walking into a house full of people sitting in a very dark reality. As always, my brother was there to yet again, pick me up and carry me through what seemed to be something I could not live through. He was feeling the same type of pain. It was different because it was his oldest niece, but still was the type of pain that my husband and I were feeling as parents and his only nephew and younger niece were also experiencing. There was nothing they could say to take any of the pain away. They were there to help carry the burden, the sorrow, the tears, the anger, and an overwhelming feeling that was crippling our thought process and emotions. They could not say anything that would take this away, but they were there to listen, hug us, cry with us, wipe our tears, and just love us through this tragedy. As the days went on, during a quiet conversation with my brother, I said to him, "I am going to write a book about things you should and shouldn't say or do for people that were grieving". I vividly remember him looking at me and saying, "I know an author that would love to help you", and that is where this book began.

I know that Haley would be super proud of us for working together to try and put down on paper something that might help someone else. Those that knew her could comprehend that she was one person on earth that you could call anytime of the day or night, and she would be there for you. Her mission in life was to "serve and help others" and that is exactly what she did all the way until the minute she left the earth. Not only would this book make her proud because of the premise that created it, but she would be proud because she was an avid reader, loved to read, and she read everything. If she was noticeably quiet, it was a sure fact she was reading a book.

One of the biggest things we learned is that we could not fix anything. As you walk through the chapters that follow, we strongly suggest that the first thing you consider is that *you cannot fix anything*. Everything that is laid before you is what has already happened. The person who has suffered the loss and is grieving cannot be repaired, at least not completely. They have lost something special and amazing. It is not coming back no matter how much they wish for it. As you consider how to communicate it is imperative that you realize this. We have stuck our

4

foot in our mouths many dozens of times and perhaps even more. You don't need to look far to understand that we all do sometimes.

As you read through this book understand that we took great care writing this together, but you will see it from two different points of view. Some of the book was written as us and some was written through our personal experiences with grief. We have read through this as a team multiple times to try to give you a positive experience in this difficult time.

Take your time, read through the writings that follow and understand we did this for Haley, we did this for ourselves, and believe it or not, we did this for you.

Part 1: The not so Positives

Ever play ping pong? When we started writing this book, we had a relatively clear idea of how we were going to approach it. The idea revolved around all the things that were said during our grieving process to us that were not so good, didn't help us, or seemed a little insensitive. I guess you could call these the "not so positive responses" and they became the basis for how we were writing. You know what they say about the best laid plans.

As we continued writing we realized you could not have the negatives without pointing out the positives. There were so many of those as well and we knew that the "positives" would help just as much as the "not so positives". Then we considered "what if that person has their feelings hurt by knowing they said one of these things that we considered negative?" Then we thought "shouldn't we be trying to help people that are dealing with the same situation?" Pondering for a little while, we thought "shouldn't we be softer in our approach?" Then it became the opposite, "shouldn't we be more direct in our approach?" By that time, we were ready to pull out our hair and go bald. We realized we had to make some decisions and put a stake in the ground.

In the end there are always questions that we must answer of ourselves and of other people. We decided to approach both the positives and the negatives with the negatives first. The idea was to avoid some of the things that could be potentially hurtful and then give reasons why we feel avoiding them was a good idea. These are from our own experience or someone that we have talked with on occasion. We also decided, what was not so positive for us, might be positive for someone else. We humbly state these are just our own findings and opinions based on our situation. We have found from talking with others and from our own experiences, knowing what to do or not to do, what to say or not to say, seems to be a struggle for most people. Helping someone who is grieving can be a tough place to be and many people would rather not have to be there. If they do feel compelled to be there with those grieving, they many times don't know what to do or say.

As we approached the more positive solutions, we could also give reasons and explanations while having already set a foundation to avoid the negatives, because they are already out there. Step one should always be to avoid the negatives as much as possible. Step two should be to look for the positives and apply them when the time is right.

We know that each of you reading have taken the first step and instead of just jumping in and saying "I know exactly what to say or do" you will instead pay attention to learn and potentially see a bigger picture of how a grieving person is feeling. We hope you learn our version of what could or could not help a person who is grieving. Just learning a few things that gave us comfort during these difficult times could potentially help you now or in the future. We too, after having to go through it ourselves, will be better equipped to help others when they are grieving or faced with difficult circumstances. We also realize we are growing constantly through the creation of this book as we write, read, edit, and are passionately involved with every word.

You may be wondering why focus on negatives or positives at all when they can sometimes be interchangeable. The reason is fairly simple. There are certain global statements that can usually be taken as a negative and in those we at least want you to think about the potential effect they can have on a person who is grieving. We also acknowledge that many things that we will be writing about may not be how some people feel. (We have and will continue to say that.) It may be that a "not so positive" statement is what someone genuinely believes and what they feel they truly need to say. In that case at least we've given them the opportunity to temper or to listen a little further before they address a grieving person.

We know that there are a lot of people that are so adamant in their beliefs that they won't necessarily pay attention to those things pointed out as potentially negative. This is especially true with some of the statements that revolve around religion. We are both very spiritual and would never set religion aside. We both felt a series of difficult emotions during our grieving process point out that using religion as a foundation may not be a direction to take early in the grieving process. There will be a time to share your beliefs that might help someone during the grieving process. Ask yourself: "Is this the time?", "Will this make them feel any better?", "Will this remove any of their pain?", "Should I just wait and share this with them when they can actually hear what I am saying?", and "Will they be able to accept what I am trying to share with them." There is an old saying that has been shared for many generations that still stands true today, "There is a time and a place for everything."

Take a moment and take inventory of your positives and negatives and how you would approach each one. As you read the text try to understand not only what the speaker was saying but how it could be interpreted by someone who is grieving. By doing this you can exercise your mind and imagination and, in the process, determine if we have pointed out the negatives you would have pointed out and vice versa.

Now take a moment and journey with us to a world that is not as positive as many people think nor as negative as others may consider. Let's take a moment and look at the things we should not say to a person who is grieving.

What Happened?

Curiosity is at the core of who we are each day. The greatest inventions of mankind have been made from the curious. Those people who seek out the truth with the tenacity that only a few understand. Often those people are oblivious to the situations around them and often curiosity can lead to misunderstanding without patience and poise.

Grief is the ultimate mystery and something that more and more people try to figure out and understand. Every single person grieves in their own way, which is expected and acceptable. One person may handle it differently than the person next to them. One thing is for sure, grief is a component that can be debilitating, exhausting, and comes and goes on its own timeline. As many people told us at the very beginning, it is like the ocean; it will come in waves. Sometimes it will be gigantic waves that will knock your feet out from under as you are just trying to "stay above water, without drowning". Other times the waves will hit you, but you can keep your footing while still feeling the waves continuously pummeling you. Then you have the waves that will come but are not as powerful and you are able to survive them with just a small stumble while still being able move forward. Grief can be triggered by a sound, a word, a song, a picture, a memory, and so much more. It is as real as the air we breathe and influences our feelings, always.

Still as you communicate with someone who is grieving, curiosity should not be at play. You may have questions and concerns. You may be a lifetime friend or a new acquaintance but your insatiable need to know details should be resolved independently. In most cases, you can do enough research and find the details you feel the need to know long before you're in the presence of those that are grieving. When it comes to the grieving, we recommend you leave the questions at home. They just add stress.

At the Church:

"As I stood in the church greeting hundreds of people and hearing some of the sweetest, most compassionate stories about how our daughter had touched someone's life, how she had made them laugh, how she had done something spectacular, and even something I considered very "Haley like" I was at ease. These stories were good for the soul.

Some of the people were quiet, patiently waiting to speak, and then speaking with deliberate caution.

Some of the people were more gregarious, full of great energy despite the situation. They filled me with life as they shared their points of view, their stories, and their love for our daughter.

Some of the people just cried for a moment, held me, and moved on. They too had suffered a great loss, they too felt at least some of my deep and unending pain. They too were grieving with me and for me.

At one point someone decided that hugging us and allowing us to cry wasn't what they needed, they needed more. They proceeded into a small conversation that was lead with a question I had dreaded and avoided for a week now, "What happened?"

I was stunned, shocked, dismayed, and honestly lost in the miasmic words that had been spoken. In my disbelief that I was being asked this, I quickly shook my head. I couldn't and didn't want to go there. The pain was so deep and so real that it struck me as though I was hit by a solid object. They wanted details of what happened on the worst day of our lives.

At no point during this day was I expecting to answer this question. Honestly, it would take virtually no effort to research exactly what happened. I felt as though everyone should know the emotions that I was feeling. I was being asked this question on the day we were here to celebrate her life and all the amazing things she had done in her short twenty-five years. It saddened me even more to contemplate facing this question again.

I shook my head and cried. I could not find any words through my renewed grief and instead said nothing.

As that person walked away, I thought to myself that if anyone needed to know what happened they should have done their research or sought others that knew the situation instead of asking me. If those events were so important to them, I was not the right source. I was the grieving mother. My advice to anyone that is seeing someone that is grieving is:

"Don't ask the grieving loved ones what happened. They will relive this series of events forever. Having to revisit that in a conversation with anyone that is there to pay their respects should never happen. It's reality to those grieving. Seek out your answers in other places."

She's in a better place

This is a statement that has been used many times when we are talking about a loved one no longer living here on earth. It's a statement that is commonly used when the loved one has suffered. In that case, stating that he or she is in a better place might be very comforting to those that are grieving. It might even bring some peace to them as they grieve because they never wanted to see their loved one suffer or even struggle. The truth is, if you know your loved one is a Christian, the Bible tells us they are in a much better place. A place that is filled with happiness and joy. Where their bodies are renewed, there is no pain, no hurt, and they are freed of any malady they were fighting. Sharing with the grieving that their loved one is pain free and no longer struggling and that they are in a better place may be received in a way that can bring them comfort.

However, when there is grief due to a tragedy it's probably not a time to share that "they are in a better place". When tragedies happen, it is unexpected and usually very devasting to their loved ones. Stating to these people that he or she is in a better place probably won't be received very well. It's different, it's shocking, and can potentially be a little offensive. Thinking of the situation and the reason the people are grieving is the key to understanding when you should make statements such as this one. Consider how you would feel if you had experienced the same and make good decisions on how to approach the grieving.

Sometimes timing can be everything. To us this is a prime example of "there is a time and a place for everything" and you just need to know when it's too soon, or if saying this causes more pain. You might just want to keep this thought to yourself. Perhaps you can share it later when the time is right, when the family can begin to consider this. Being aware of what you are saying to those grieving so deeply, can help avoid hurt feelings and more pain for your loved ones.

Visitation Line:

As I was standing in the visitation line for hours, I heard so many things. People just wanted to be able to say something that would ease my pain and the pain of my family. They were standing in a line for quite some time waiting to share their special story, give us a hug, share some of our tears, show love, and give their best effort to take a piece of our pain away. As one person gave me a hug and looked into my eyes, they said "she's in a better place".

There is no doubt in my mind that she is in a better place but there is not one part of that statement that made me or my family feel any better at that moment. I don't know a parent that has experienced a tragic experience like ours that wants to hear that their child, who is no longer here with them on this earth, whom they will not get to physically see, hug, laugh with, cry with, and grow older with is in a better place.

It didn't help us at that moment and in most similar cases, wouldn't help anyone at all. Instead, it actually made it hurt a little more. We as parents want to think that our home, where we loved her so very much, was the best place for her to be. We didn't want to even consider that she was anywhere but here with us. It was painful.

There are some things that can just be said too soon, way before those hearing it can even comprehend it. Even now, I wish she were here on earth with us. I wish we had more time with her. Do I know that she is in a better place? YES. Did I need to hear that at any point during this initial grieving period? NO. Did I need to hear it while standing in the visitation line? NO.

Some families may never want to hear that, it may take years for them to come to terms with that idea, if ever. Some people know it is true, but they too don't want to hear it. I will tell you in our case, a tragic accident, hearing that "she is in a better place" during the grieving process did not bring anything but more hurt and tears at that time. Maybe this was something that could have been saved for a better time because we only wanted her to be with us, right then, and to not be facing the grief we were feeling.

God needed her more

As people grieve it is hard to determine what should be said or done. Most people speak from their heart and genuinely want to share something with you to make sense of the unsensible. They want to share something uplifting, or just a word or two that will remove at least an ounce of your pain. It is extremely easy to go to words that you have been told, you have heard repeatedly, or that you have read in scripture.

It is hard to know what to say when you witness someone in the valleys of grief and it's easy to regurgitate what has been shared by others on previous occasions. It's a fact that there are scriptures after scriptures that confirm many of these statements, quotes, or even sayings and those are 100% true. They are backed up and confirmed by tomes of scholars and clergy and have been used for quite some time.

The question is, when do you share these types of things or should you even share them at all? When will the grieving person be able to accept this information? When will it help them, or will it ever help them? You are determining when and how to deliver this information

Before breaking out scripture on a grieving family or individual you need to make sure you know if it applies and that it is accurate for the context. Did you in fact read the passage and the passages before it and after it? Is it really speaking to those grieving?   Is this really what the Bible says or is this just something you have heard others say?

People have strong beliefs and during a time where the biggest question is "Why?" religion can often play the "go to" part. Make sure you check your resources and that you are speaking the truth. No matter what your beliefs, if you have any inkling towards God, then you will often find yourself looking to the Heavens for answers. If you have strong Christian beliefs, it is easy to rationalize that God is in control no matter what. You must remember that the people who are grieving might not be ready to accept what the scripture says, they might be so far in the depth of grief they can't even fathom what you are sharing. You might miss your opportunity to help someone that needs to hear your scripture if you choose to deliver it before they are truly ready.

You also need to make sure that what you choose to share with them is something that will actually help them during this time of grieving. Even if it is the truth, will it help right now? When a person experiences extreme grief or has an intense personal loss in their heart, some people, thinking they want to help, will explain an unknown situation as God's will. They also may share scripture with you, which can be completely written in the Bible, but it might not be the right time for those grieving to listen.

When saying "God needed them more" it seems as if you are placing the blame on God and you are asking those that are grieving to feel better because God needed them. It's doesn't allow those grieving to have the right to grieve because you have now blamed God for taking them. This statement needs to be avoided until those grieving can hear it the way that you intend it. It also can make those that are grieving feel selfish for wanting their loved one even though what you are saying is that God needed them more.

As you struggle to find meaning I hope, and yes, I pray that you can find solace in your mind that there was a reason for God to allow the situation that happened. I strongly suggest and even passionately plea that you avoid relaying that opinion to the recently grieving. Suggesting that their loss was someone else's gain even if it is the almighty God may not only cause more pain but also create conflict in a grieving persons mind. As your mind rationalizes the comfort it may bring the grieving, they may struggle to understand why the incredible pain they are feeling would be inflicted upon them by a loving God.

Sharing these parts of the scripture does not help everyone and it might depend on where they are in the grieving process. Trust me, the pain is very real, and it does not go away easily. In most cases it will never fully go away. Depending on where they are in the grieving process, what you share with them may hurt more than it helps. The intent of some people as they witness those who are grieving is to try to "fix it". They may want to say something that will allow those that are grieving to feel relieved or comforted. Unfortunately, the truth is, there is NOTHING you can say that will take away the pain of those grieving. If they have lost a loved one here on earth, it is just painful. Whether it was something they predicted was going to happen or was a tragic event that allowed no preparation, it is still painful. You cannot fix it for them. You can comfort them, love, and support them, but you can't fix it and the quicker you realize you can't fix it, and realize in most cases anything you say may not help the pain, the better it will be. Allowing people to grieve is what is needed. They need to grieve, and they need room to deal with their feelings and emotions. Make sure that you are encouraging the grieving and not trying to get them to "move on" too quickly. Don't dismiss their grieving, just walk along side of them.

First Days:

We had just been thrown into the worst night of our lives and now, upon daylight, we were facing an even more difficult morning. People have now been told about our situation and everyone is trying to figure out what to do and say in our uncharted time. People were looking to say something that would make some semblance of sense to themselves and to us. With that in mind, many went to scripture or to a passage they had read or heard in the past to try to give us some comfort.

I clearly remember that someone came into our house the morning after the accident and stated that "God needed her more than you did". I didn't need to hear that; it didn't help me or my family make rhyme or reason of the situation. Instead, it actually made me stop and think about all that I knew to be true. Saying that God needed her more was not a way to make me feel any better and made me question my core beliefs. The pain was so fresh and deep that thinking that God took our daughter to Heaven because he needed her just didn't make any sense in a situation that already didn't make any sense.

I remember thinking that if this is true, all the things I have been told, studied, read, and been taught my entire life about God would have been lies. I knew that wasn't true because what I did know was that God didn't need our daughter more than we did. According to what I have read in the Bible, God is a BIG God, and he doesn't need anyone for anything. He is fully capable of handling everything on his own. He didn't need her. Though we know our sweet daughter is in Heaven it's not because God needed her. Again, it seems as though this person was trying to blame God.

Yes, I think people want to say something that will make sense of a situation but claiming that God needed my daughter more, just doesn't make any sense. It doesn't go along with what the Bible really says. It seems to be a cliché' that people use during an extremely uncomfortable situation.

According to the Bible, Heaven is a glorious place where there are no tears, no sorrow, and no pain. I am certain God doesn't need children or young adults to be there. Of course, I know there are children and young adults that go to Heaven every day. I know these children go because of unfortunate circumstances. Still, I don't believe that God takes them from earth because he needs them in Heaven. I believe God is an almighty God that doesn't need anyone and is fully capable of doing anything and everything. For someone to say that he needed our daughter in Heaven shouldn't have been shared with me, a grieving mother. Think about it, if you believe in God, I can tell you, based on my studies, that he doesn't "need" anyone in Heaven. I know that he's "got this" and has complete control of everything. To me it sounded like they were pointing fingers at God for my situation. It dismissed my feelings as I was grieving and the process I was and am still going through. Worse, it made me question a lot of things. This is something I shouldn't have had to worry about during that time.

God knew

Predestiny has been debated since the dawn of time. We cannot really get into that type of debate here as it would take books upon books of point and counterpoint. Instead let's consider for a moment the idea of predestiny when you are dealing with someone who is grieving. It's really easy to come up with a statement that says that all of this was meant to be. People consider it all the time. They look for reasons and they are consistently looking for answers on that ever-present question, "Why?".

When you start talking about "God's Plan" for someone life, people tend to quote things from the Bible, yet again. The most commonly used one is Jeremiah 29:11 "For I know the plans I have for you, declares the Lord, plans for welfare and not for evil, to give you a future and a hope". What people don't say is that this was spoken to the entire Jewish population living in Babylon. This wasn't spoken to an individual.

Stating that God had a plan for those that are suffering or grieving just doesn't help them. It makes them feel powerless. People often feel powerless already when they are grieving.

If you take a moment and search the Internet, you will find hundreds of pros and cons on the idea of predestiny. There is a great deal of information supporting predestiny from The Bible and just as much against predestiny from, of course, The Bible. It can easily be said that you could debate yourself as much as you could any person on whether there is Free Will. It could also be said that God has planned every moment of your life down to the last second and when things happen it is because it has been "planned out". Talking about "God's plan" during the crisis or even while the person is grieving should be avoided.

Free Will is another debatable concept that people feel one way or the other about. Thinking that our choices lead to a logical end is also something that a grieving person does not need to hear. Consider Free Will as a series of decisions about something much different than life or death. It may be true that our Free Will leads to a conclusion but stating that one decision or another can cause such grief is insensitive and should be avoided. Yes, you have the Free Will to eat something that "could" cause an illness or do something that has been proven to cause an illness, however it's usually not Free Will to be in a tragic accident. Sometimes people are trying to find someone to blame so if they state that a person had Free Will to get in their car one evening that resulted in a tragic accident, it allows them to lay blame on those that had Free Will. God, who loves his children, would not prescribe to this type of Free Will. People sometimes like to say these things to make themselves feel better or to find an answer for the grieving. It is not a good answer.

When someone is grieving their mind is experiencing sensory overload. It's not just that they've experienced some type of loss it is also that they are replaying moment after moment of their interactions with that special person. Their mind becomes fuzzy as more and more items are forced into their line of thought and along the way it adds even more to an already stressed system. The end result is an overwhelming feeling that cascades and, in the end, causes even more overthinking.

As you are considering your approach to talking to someone who is grieving take a moment and set the predestiny line of thinking aside. It may be your attempt to comfort someone, but it may only cause more confusion, frustration, and overthinking as to the "why".

God knows:

I believe that God knows everything. That is not what I am disputing here, but I cannot figure out how telling a grieving loved one that "God knew when he put her on earth, when he was going to take her" was going to help me at all. Yes, they were stating a fact that many would believe to be true and were attempting to take some of the pain away. I understood that they were trying to help me, the grieving mother, but telling me this didn't really comfort me at all. It was yet another thing that people tend to say in a difficult situation. It might have been because they had heard it said before, or maybe it was what they believed, or maybe they were trying to "fix it" and in the process fix me. It was a statement that didn't help me, nor did it fix any part of my broken heart.

I remember being in my home as people were coming in and out, bringing food, flowers, and gifts. All the while they were hugging and crying with each of us. I was surrounded by loved ones, both family and friends, and I remember just being so sad and so devastated. Mostly I remember crying uncontrollably a majority of the time. In the midst of this I remember someone was there to share their condolences and while doing so decided to announce to me that "God knew when he put her on earth the day he was going to take her".

I am still not sure how any of that information was helpful to a grieving mother who had just realized she would never see her daughter here on earth again. Maybe God does know when he puts you on earth, the day you will join him in Heaven. I promise you that to hear someone say those words didn't help my broken heart at all. Quite frankly, it made me mad and even more sad. This person should have considered asking themselves, "Will the statement I am getting ready to make, help her as she is hurting so badly?". If the answer was "I don't know", "No", "Maybe" or anything but absolutely yes, they should not have said it. Maybe not then, maybe not ever.

The statement may be true. I really don't know for sure. It was, however, not the appropriate time or place to share it. It had been weeks since our daughter went to Heaven when I wrote this and when I think about that statement, it still upsets me. I believe that God knows everything that happens here on earth but having someone tell me this, did not help me at all. It just broke my heart a little more.

You and your spouse will need counseling.

We inferred and actually said in the introduction that we were not license doctors or psychologists. Both of us have experienced a tremendous amount in our lives and have talked over the years with a great deal of seriousness about our incredibly unique childhood. It is always interesting when we are talking to each other how we perceive life and the positive paths that we have both taken even though our childhoods, or should I say childhood, was filled with constant conflict and a lot of things that many people today would have a difficult time facing.

One of the things that we found was that we could always count on each other even though sometimes that meant we were at odds for a while. I remember the two of us talking about our conflicts that were relatively constant and concluding that our conflicts allowed us to work items out in a safe environment. Still, even we, as brother and sister had lines that we did not cross and paid careful attention to each other even under the veil of conflict. In the end, we knew what lines not to cross and we always paid attention to the other feelings.

When you consider someone who is already dealing with an exceedingly difficult situation or who are emotionally compromised in some way it's not exactly the best idea to stoke fuel on that fire? Telling someone things like "these things always happen in threes", or "bad things happen to good people", or "she's in a better place" borderlines on difficulty and even touches cruelty. This is true even if you are just trying to help. These types of statements don't really help those who are grieving, they are just opinions coming from those that are standing on the outside.

Telling someone they need counseling is a time sensitive statement and in the midst of their initial grief may be too soon to consider. Are you qualified to say that? Are you a counselor? If you are a counselor, are you too close to the people to make that statement?

Consider for a moment your words and your qualifications. Consider for a moment who you are talking to at that time. Before you make a recommendation make sure that it's something that is going to help and not cause additional pain or issues. Make sure your statement is timed correctly as well as correct.

We know this may sound repetitive. We have said "Consider who you are talking to" and "know where they are in the grieving process" numerous times already in this book and will continue to say it. This is at the core of dealing with people in a grieving situation. Always consider the situation before you speak or act.

Counseling:

We now know statistics say that many marriages struggle when a child is taken from earth. Sharing that with us during the first couple of days caused a tremendous amount of stress that was unnecessary. Not only were we trying to come to terms with the reality that our sweet daughter was no longer here on earth and what had happened to our family as we knew it. We were now thrown into worrying about what could happen to our marriage and if it was going to struggle or even fail.

I saw this as a "kick them when they are down" scenario. We were already dealing with enough and now having to worry about something we really didn't need to worry about a few days after the accident, was uncalled for and a worry that could have been avoided.

We had multiple people share their thoughts about counseling and the pressure of grief on our marriage. Some of the shared thoughts were how much counseling helped them during an exceedingly difficult time in their life. They also pointed out how much counseling can be a place to have an outsider help steer you as you navigate through these unfamiliar territories. Some people would mention a great counselor's name they knew or would send us contact information for a great counselor that they highly recommended.

I remember someone coming in asking me if we were planning to do counseling. This will not surprise anyone that knows me well, I commented with a little sarcasm "I needed counseling long before now, so Yes, we will seek counseling very soon."

22

This person then proceeded to share with me that our marriage had a good chance of struggling or failing because "it happens to people that lose a child." I remember getting an extremely sick feeling in my stomach because I would now have to worry about not only all that my family was going through but also about my marriage. That evening I remember going to my husband who was also drowning in sadness, sorrow, and grief, to tell him what had been said to me. I told him how I now had more to worry about moving forward. This was presented to me as "your marriage will struggle" instead of "counselling helped me" or "I know a great counselor if you want someone to talk to, to help all of you". Now I had to shift some of my focus to negate these types of thoughts. Stacy, my husband, and I neither one wanted to or should have had to worry about our marriage while we were suffering and dealing with this tragic accident. We needed to be able to love and support each other. We needed be able to give that love and support not only to each other but to our children. In doing so we needed to show our children how we can all attempt to handle things when life is tough or in this case almost unmanageable. We did not and should not have had to worry about our marriage.

We have now been told this same thing a few different times. We both realize that going through this is hard on everyone and it puts stress on not only your health and wellbeing but also your marriage and relationships with friend and family. Those are true facts but keeping an open line of communication with your spouse and knowing that everyone will grieve differently is a key to helping our marriage stay healthy. I feel that counseling for both parents is also highly recommended. It's a good place for anyone to "unload" in a safe place and have someone help them navigate through their feeling and grief. I am not saying that people's marriages do not struggle during stressful situations. When people are in deep grief it does cause tremendous amounts of stress, and that can result in people struggling personally which can cause your relationships to struggle. What I am suggesting is that you offer a good counselor but don't interject your feelings about failure or strife. Instead focus on the positives and helping people along.

If you feel strongly about it, try waiting a little while and then giving them a name of a good counselor stating, "in case you feel you need someone to talk to." You can also share a story of someone that had counseling, perhaps yourself, and how it helped.

God never gives you more than you can handle.

How many times have you heard this in your lifetime? People say all the time "God never gives you more than you can handle". They say this no matter what the situation is, no matter how big or small the struggle is, or what problem is being faced. It's certainly a "go to" phrase and obviously overused. Some would argue that 1 Corinthians 10:13 teaches "God won't give you more than you can handle" however this complete verse states "No temptation has overtaken you except what is common to mankind. And God is faithful; he will not let you be tempted beyond what you can bear. But when you are tempted, he will also provide a way out so that you can endure it." People that use this phrase and base it on 1 Corinthians 10:13 might be explaining that the word temptation can refer to suffering. We don't think that Paul was referring to suffering when he was addressing sin. If you have lost a loved one, especially one that is taken unexpectedly or tragically, the emotion that is attached is more than some people can handle. Maybe it is more than most people can handle. Sharing this phrase may hold no weight with referencing the teachings of Bible, in our opinion.

Each and every day we are challenged with the directions we must take. Often, we are challenged with incredible obstacles and near impossible tasks. One of the quotes that we have laughed about over and over to people has always been "it is said the good Lord never gives you more than you can handle, but I surely wish he would stop thinking so highly of me."

When it comes to grief the challenges are honestly incredible and potentially near insurmountable. As you are considering the grieving people that you are about to engage, you need to consider the path they're taking. If you think about it, many of us are trying to determine a way to talk to someone who has potentially lost their way. You're going to try to comfort someone who potentially can see no easy path to success or to even feeling better.

We have said a great many people have considerable faith and, in that faith, they focus on what they believe. Often this is what is taught by the church but sometimes it is based on interaction with others or their interpretation of a scripture or sermon. We are also often contemplating how we are perceived by God. This contemplation adds credibility to who we are but also can add confusion or frustration.

We are not trying in any way to dissuade anyone from any type of religion. We are both quite spiritual and were brought up in in a strong church environment. This environment lead each of us a different way and as we reviewed it with each other over the years we realized that although our foundations were similar, we had grown and interpreted things differently, but ended up in a similar state after we found our ways.

As we were writing this book together, we continued to discover a lot more about each other and how we felt about things. These are items that rarely got discussed at the kitchen table and when they did there were sometimes disagreements, so we just avoided it. Still, it was there and at the core were a significant number of beliefs imparted by our grandparents and others in our lives.

A misnomer that we faced was the idea that the good Lord never gives you more than you can handle. Many, including us, have used this over and over to downplay a critical set of issues. Often when you consider this idea, you have to wonder just how difficult it can be to determine how much someone can actually handle. You have to determine when they can handle what they are facing and more importantly when being there for them is necessary. We would like to suggest that perhaps stating that "The good Lord never gives you more than you can handle" is a statement you should use with careful consideration. If you think about it, you understand that many wish that he would stop thinking so highly of them and instead ease off a little.

Still, and more importantly, if you consider what a parent, friend, husband, wife, father, child, or any other close friend or relative goes through in such a difficult time, you may change your approach. If you say this to someone you should quickly realize it is like putting a 15th book on a librarian's stack they are carrying to the shelves and wondering if they will make it. Will they make it, or will the stack fall? The question is the same when people are dealing with grief. As more and more are added to their "stack" it can be exceedingly difficult to comprehend how much more they can handle, and you have to be aware the "stack" may be too heavy to carry alone.

Sweet Friend:

I was meeting with a sweet friend who had lost her son a few years ago. We were discussing things that people had done to support us and things we would never forget. We both agreed and acknowledged that that people's intentions, no matter what they said or did, came from the heart and it was out of pure goodness and love. As we discussed some of the things we had been told we both brought up the phrase "God only gives you what you can handle". We both had heard that a few different times during our grieving process. We agreed when people would say that it didn't really make sense. We both felt it wasn't true. As grieving moms, we were overwhelmed with emotion and every moment was too much to handle. We also agreed the situation was too much every second of every day.

Even today, there are days, it still feels like it is too much to handle. I knew I had been pushed beyond what I could deal with, which is why I could not make decisions, didn't have an appetite, couldn't sleep at night, couldn't get up in the morning, and why my emotions were always running so high. It took months to even begin to handle daily life. I was right in the midst of grieving and was confident that I was way beyond what I could handle at the time. Stating that God wouldn't give me more than I could handle, just wasn't the truth. If this was true, he thought very highly of me and right at that time I didn't feel the same way.

Just push through it

There are lots of examples in everyday literature of heroes and heroines that find deep strength inside of themselves and push through. You don't have to look far to find that person who is more than willing to "find a way" through the impossible.

Sometimes though it seems almost impossible when facing grief or severe loss. The impossible may be exactly what everything is at the time it is happening. As we've stated before a person going through grief may have dozens of different thoughts at once making things blurry and keeping them from seeing as clearly as they normally would. It should be noted that getting through the day may be more to them than the average observer could possibly understand.

If you encounter someone who has severe grief or has just experienced an exceedingly difficult situation, consider your method prior to making a statement about how they should approach their situation. As you walk into their presence, even if you have experienced similar grief, remember you have not experienced the same thing nor have your life experiences matched up exactly with the person in front of you. Telling them to "push through" or to "find a way" may make a lot of sense to you but it could possibly make absolutely no sense to them. To be perfectly clear they may be "pushing through" just to be talking to you and they may be experiencing severe emotions while appearing to just be slightly upset.

"Finding a way" can be extremely hard when you have been put to a test in which you don't know how you can even think about tomorrow. Stating you'll "find a way" to a person who is grieving, whether they have lost someone or experienced anything that has caused them great amounts of grief, may not be accepted well. They most likely will need help getting to that point and having love and support is really the thing they need the most. In our opinion, most people don't understand that grieving is something that you may do or will do for the rest of your life. You may manage it differently as you go on, but you might not ever stop grieving. Telling someone that they will "find a way" to make it through, is a lot easier said than done and grief is something that can creep up on you in a matter of seconds, when you least expect it. It might be triggered by something that is said or something that happens, that takes you right back to your grieving spot. Instead of encouraging them to "find a way" just love them through the grieving process. Support them and try to understand that grief comes in "waves" and sometimes you don't even know you are getting ready to be hit by this wave of emotion at that time. No matter the amount of time that you have had to prepare for a loved one to die or something bad to happen, the grief turns out to be 1,000 times worse than you expected. Even if you know a loved one is not suffering or in pain any longer, it still doesn't change the fact that you are without them here physically on earth. Let those that are grieving, grieve. Let them have their time and space if needed to just grieve. Grief is such a unique thing and as much as you prepare, it's still extremely hard to handle at times.

Loving our Children:

I think most people have no idea what it's like to lose a child. Up to this point, their lives haven't been touched by a loss of this magnitude. They might have lost someone very dear to them, in fact most people have done that, but to have to bury a child is one of the worse things a parent can endure.

I say all the time, until you have walked in these shoes, you really have no idea of the pain that is associated to losing a child. My husband and I say all the time, "we love our kids so hard". We have loved them this way all their lives, even as young adults, we still participated in everything, they were involved in. Our daughter was in plays and musicals all her life. As she got a little older, she directed plays and we still didn't miss one of them. We went and watched even when she wasn't on stage. When she was on stage, we didn't miss a show. We saw everything. Our son played basketball throughout high school and also played in college. I remember as a freshman in college he did not get a lot of playing time. We still went to all the home games and some of the away games. We didn't want to miss the chance to see him play, even if it was for a few seconds. Our youngest daughter is a competitive dancer, and we travel all over the place watching and supporting her and her dreams. Some people might think we are too involved or crazy but that is just how we love them and support them. We wanted to always show them, we are there to support you, no matter what it is. As is with most parents, we love our kids and quite honestly have molded our lives around their lives and activities. I would not change that for anything, and I live with no regrets because our kids were our top priority. We just made the decision that we would invest all that we had into them and their wellbeing.

It was our mission when we had children to have them love the Lord, serve others, and love each other. We wanted to teach them the importance of having each other to lean on however I wanted them all to be strong. I wanted them to stand up for what they knew was right and, as I have said to them often, to "dare to be different". I didn't want them to be a follower. I wanted them to be strong, do the right things, and to know that sometimes you just need to "pull yourself up by your bootstraps" and carry on. I wanted them to push through obstacles that got in their way that they might be confronted with each day. However, this time it was different. We were grieving, we have loss in our life, we are hurt as a family and as individuals and we were trying to just figure out how to take the next breath.

During the first week our kids had some amazing friends come to be by their side. These young people will never know how much we appreciated them coming to love and support our kids while we too needed our family and friends to love and support us. One night someone said to our daughter "just push through it". I'm sure they had been coached by someone along the way that encouraged them to "push through" the pain, or exhaustion. This was different and all I could think was they don't really expect her to just "push through it" do they? Our fifteen-year-old daughter had lost her sister, her rock, her mentor, the one that thought she hung the moon, and she was not going to "push through" this one. She, like all the rest of us, was just trying to figure out how to put one foot in front of the other.

Just "push through it" was not going to happen and, quite honestly, I didn't want her to have the pressure of just pushing through it. I wanted her to grieve, cry, yell, and be mad or sad, if that is what she was feeling, or she needed and wanted to do. I didn't want her to "push through" during this time and not grieve properly. If she just "pushed through" now in five or ten years she might experience grief that she didn't deal with today. They say there is a grieving process and in order to cope you should be allowed to go through the entire process however you see fit. With that in mind, I don't recommend telling anyone to just push through it when they are grieving. Just love them through the grieving process and be there when they are broken. Encourage them with a sweet story, a hug, a prayer, a note, or even a surprise quart of their favorite ice cream. Don't ask them to push through it, walk with them through it so that they can grieve properly, and they will never forget your kindness.

Don't Cry

One of the things that most people do when they lose someone is cry. Crying is the bodies way to express emotions. No matter if you are man or woman, young or old, crying is okay for everyone, no matter what you have been told.

Let's get a few facts here. Crying is good for you and can assist your body in a significant number of ways. Crying releases toxins that are in your body and can purge hormones that are plaguing you as much as emotional issues. Detoxifying the body is good for you. Crying for a while can get you to a point that you don't need to cry anymore as it helps you cope emotionally. It helps to self soothe and is one of your best mechanisms to do so. It causes you to breathe and breathing is the center of life. Think about when babies are born, the doctors want them to cry which helps them breathe. Crying can improve your mood and help you while you are grieving. Crying informs others that you may be in distress and it is recognized by nearly every culture as an emotional center to rally around. Crying can help you sleep and can exhaust you to the point that you can relax. It helps restore emotional balance. Some researchers even believe that crying helps your nervous system deal with pain either emotional or physical. Sounds like crying isn't too bad for you.

Even if people don't always believe it there are lots of benefits to crying. Still society has a tendency to look down upon crying and in many cases crying makes people uncomfortable. When we were younger, we would do almost anything to stop each other from crying. Not because we didn't want to get into trouble but instead, we wanted each other to be happy.

Telling someone to hide their emotions and not to cry, could make a person suppress their true feelings to avoid making people uncomfortable. Telling someone not to cry also can cause the person to feel guilty, which negates their feelings. Crying is a healthy way of expressing what they are experiencing at this moment in time. Keeping emotions bottled up inside can build up and cause harm, anger, depression and more, later in life. Feelings that are not expressed in a healthy way usually creep out later and could be shared in a not so healthy way. Asking someone not to cry is keeping them from doing something that is natural.

One of the early lessons that we learned during this process was that saying "don't cry" never seemed to have that effect. Instead saying "don't cry" could often elicit the most massive crying that could instantly break glass in the area and potentially cause birds and small planes to fall out of the sky. Still many people take that approach when they see someone crying. Instead of trying to understand the how's and the why's of crying they just want it to stop. Doing so can often be a mistake or worse make people cry more.

As with most of the items that we have talked about we really need to consider when we walk into a room what we should be doing. If you see someone crying, step down and hold them and try to make it better or offer comfort. Consider just listening or better yet just crying with the person who needs you. Telling them to stop crying will not address any of their issues or make things any better for them. It might even make things worse.

Not Ashamed:

In normal circumstances, those at our house are not big criers. My girls and I don't cry over movies, books, or shows most of the time. We cry when people we love are hurting but we don't get emotional. We don't cry a lot even when we are angry unless it's very bad, and then it seems we come unglued.

I think some people are just natural criers, their emotions are different than mine, they feel differently than I do. I'm not ashamed to cry, it just doesn't come easy for me. Maybe it was my upbring or the circumstances I faced that makes it difficult for me to cry.

I found, however, that when deep grief happens, you are overwhelmed with tears. As I am writing this, we still cry every single day. We cry when we talk about Haley, we cry when we talk to people about things she won't get to experience, or things she did experience. We cry because we miss her, we cry because we love her dearly. We cry when someone else is crying and grieving for us. Our friends and family cry. I have seen my husband fall to his knees and cry. My son and daughter cry to the point of exhaustion. We lay awake at night and cry; we wake and cry. We see our kids crying because they miss Haley, then we begin to cry with them.

We cry and it's okay. God gave us emotions and the ability to cry. Every bit of that is okay. I am sure that people don't like to watch others cry, it is heart wrenching to see people hurt, broken, and crying. Allowing people to feel whatever emotion it is that they are feeling is healthy and people encouraging any and all of them to do so is good for those grieving.

One of the things I remember the most about the first couple of days was I cried all day, every day. I could not control my emotions; people were coming in and out of our house and when I would see them, I would cry because most of them were crying too. They were crying because they saw us in so much pain and they also hurt because of what had happened. We were the saddest we had ever been, and they too were sad. People were crying because we were so broken, and I genuinely believe they cried because they could feel some of the pain we were enduring. They couldn't by any means, feel the exact pain we felt but they could see the pain we were going through, and they just cried with us.

I remember some of my friends coming into the house and approaching me. I would take the time to just glance their way, they could see my pain and would just cry. There was NOTHING you could say that would make this any better or change the circumstances. It was ok to just cry with us. It showed us that you too were vulnerable and that you were acknowledging the pain, tears, and struggles we were going through. Those are things I will never forget.

My parents had come to be with us. My stepmother knew exactly where I was as she too had lost a daughter and was now grieving for the loss of her granddaughter. She came looking for me one morning and found me in my closet laying on the floor. The burden was too heavy for me to carry that day, the pain was too much, and I remember her laying down beside me on the closet floor and just crying along side of me. We did not say a word, we were just sharing the tears and hoping to hold onto the love through this moment in time.

I remember those girl friends that are a lot like me, they aren't natural criers, and they would sit beside me, holding my hand and they would cry with me. Most were not saying anything, just sharing the heart filled tears that were flowing from our faces. I am glad that they didn't say "don't cry" because I needed to cry. I needed to fall apart, I needed to be covered up with support and love and more importantly, I needed people to share my agony and just cry with me.

My brother and sister-in-law, my niece and her husband, my sister in laws, my parents, my best friends, my neighbors, my co-workers, my bosses, my former employers, my daughter's and my son's friends and their parents, just cried with us day after day. They still cry with us even now. They never said, "don't cry", they just cried with us or held us up while we cried. It's what makes humanity so amazing. You feel emotion when you see someone you love or care about, struggling. I say CRY, no matter if you are a man or a woman, young or old, it's okay to cry, it's good to cry, and when you cry with others that are hurting, it makes a mark on them that can never be taken away, it's what I needed and something I will never forget.

If you are not a crier, it's okay, but you're hugging them or being with them while they are crying is just as important, helpful, and needed. It is some peoples "go to" to say, "DON'T CRY", when someone is emotional. Asking them to not cry is either just a go to phrase again or you are asking them to not do something that they need to do. It could be greatly beneficial to them at the time. It will also allow them to process what they are feeling, maybe it will take one ounce of the pain away, or just allow them to cope at that moment. Allow them to cry. Encourage them to express their feelings. It will help them more.

Death comes in threes

This has been a statement, superstition, or something that people have been told or taught for many years. You have probably heard it a million times or at least a few dozen times. It started as a wives' tale, superstition, and has been passed along from generation to generation. However, the reality is, death doesn't come in threes they come in ones and before the year is up, there are millions of deaths each year. Even though this is a superstition or wives' tale, people tend to use this statement because it's what they've heard or maybe they have possible experienced three deaths in a row, which then seems to give some credibility to "death comes in threes".

The question here would be, when do you start to count and then start over at one? The second question would be, when does saying "death comes in threes" help anyone that is grieving? In our opinion this is a situation yet again that really won't help anyone that is grieving. The grieving ones are consumed with their own situation and usually aren't thinking about another death. When you are grieving it is really hard to add more to sort through. Your brain can only handle so much at a time while you are grieving. Sharing wives' tales, superstitions, or anything like this to those that are grieving doesn't take any of their pain away, nor does it make them feel any better. It could possibly cause them even more stress if they then have to start thinking about what number this loss would be for them. Is it 1, 2, or 3? It's not anything they should have to try and figure out because it's not factual, it's a superstition. These are things you wait and share when people are not in the midst of grieving. If you want to share your beliefs, superstitions, or old wives' tales with friends wait to be in a lighter atmosphere. As you share this wives' tale, I hope you know what number you are on. If not, it may cause more stress for everyone, including you.

Panic:

Shortly after our daughter's ceremony we still had people coming in out of our house, sharing stories, food, and memories. During a visit someone brought up that "death comes in threes", which they remembered hearing at one time. At that moment I literally thought about going into a panic as I began to worry about things I shouldn't have had to worry about. It placed additional fear in my situation, which I shouldn't have been facing at the time.

Sharing superstitions and things that have no value isn't a good idea at all. Even sharing facts sometimes doesn't have a place during the grieving process but sharing things that are made up or have no real truth have no place to be shared. We had so much already going on and adding this simple wives' tale just didn't set well with us. I continue to come back to the suggestions "sometimes just not saying much at all, is better". In this case it was definite.

I know how you feel

Comparing losses or grief situations is not something you can measure like the facts that you learned in science. You can't compare the weight or height or the amount of grief anyone is experiencing. Grief is not quantifiable, and it can't be measured by the amount of suffering or heartache that accompanies those that are grieving. People that are grieving are experiencing loss or sadness, but those experiences are all unique and they vary widely.

People say "I know how you feel" all the time. It's like a way to compare your feelings with someone else feelings. People feel that if they express that they too have felt a certain way, the one grieving will be able to see that others have felt the same pain and it could possibly help someone feel better. That's usually not the case. It actually can diminish the feelings of the grieving person. Stating that someone else's grief was more important or more difficult isn't really acknowledging their grief. This also takes the emphasis away from the grieving person who needs to be the focus.

Unless you have been through the exact same situation, saying you know how the person that is grieving feels, shouldn't be said. Yes, people that lose loved ones in their lives, experience pain. Sometimes that pain seems unbearable, but unless you have walked the exact same journey, saying you know how they feel isn't a good way to acknowledge their feelings. It will also not contribute to them feeling any better. A loss is a loss, and it elicits pain for those left on earth. Losing a parent or a grandparent, is not the same as losing a spouse, and losing a child is not the same as losing a sibling. Each of these are different and people try to compare their loss with other losses to explain that they too have felt this type of pain. The reality is, if it is not the same type of loss, it's doesn't compare. Even if the situation is similar there are a great many factors that build grief, from life experience to the relationship with your loved one.

We unfortunately do have friends that have lost children. Their pain is similar to ours, but not the exact same. They have lived in a similar situation and our guess is they will never forget that pain. It is somewhat comforting to speak to someone that has walked in your shoes. We see them and see "hope". Though a loss, no matter who it is, is a loss pain associated to that loss.

At the Church:

When we were standing at the church for hours as we greeted all the people that were attending the service, my son and I would share a sweet story someone had told us, or something that was lighthearted that someone shared. In the midst of visitation, my son Hayden walked over to me and said, "someone just came by and hugged me and said I know how you feel, I lost my dog a few months back". What we know is the person who said this had felt grief assuming they love their dog like we love our dog, however losing your dog and Hayden losing his sister were nothing alike. The pain is deep for both losses but to us there was no comparison.

What those people who have experienced extreme grief say is certainly helpful because they remember all too well the pain and devastation they felt when they experienced the same type of loss. Every loss that someone feels that causes grief is legitimate. Those feelings are real, they are valid, and certainly I can't say that one loss has more pain than another. What I do know is our loss for us was the worst pain we have ever encountered. Maybe their loss was that for them too, but every loss is different, and you should not have to or want to compare them. People compare because it makes them think they are feeling the same exact feelings, but every person is different, every pain is different, every situation is different. Don't compare.

Feelings for my Father:

I stood in front of hundreds of people I did not know. It had been a difficult week. I was not sure how I should be reacting at this point and even less sure of how my emotions were running rampant. There were many people who came up to me shook my hand and smiled saying how great my father was and many people who just nodded as they walked by me while I simply struggled with the moment.

To understand the depth of what I was feeling you have to understand that my father and I had a difficult life and were rarely in contact with each other until after I turned 16. As with so many people in today's society my sister and I were victims of a divorce and a series of less than perfect decisions that left us in chaos more than order. I am sure my facial expressions were unclear and I'm sure that I said both wrong and right things during that day.

I had spent a significant number of years trying to make things right and this process had its ups and downs. My father and I were a lot alike even though I did not grow up with him and had minimal contact. Our interactions were often pointed and sometimes we pushed each other to our limits. Still, over a long period of time we came to terms with just about everything and though there was much to still discuss our relationship became positive and our discussions even more positive.

A week before my father died, I received an email from him telling me that it was time for us to take a motorcycle ride together and to get my motorcycle ready as he would his. We had never ridden together even though both of us we're avid riders. This would be a new step for us both. Instead, a week later I was standing and greeting people who were honoring his life at his memorial service.

As I went from person to person a young woman walked up to me and shook my hand. She talked to me about all of the things that my father had talked about and about me specifically in several cases. She asked how I was doing, and my response was pretty easy "I'm just trying to get by at the moment."

Her reply was not meant with any malice, but she said to me "I know how you feel."

She went on and I continued talking to people as the long line continued to grow. It wasn't until about 5 minutes after that woman had said that I suddenly had increasing uneasiness and became a little frustrated. I was dealing with a significant amount of angst right now and it bothered me because this wasn't just about my father's death, it was about 1,000 other things that were weighing on me because of his death. On one hand I appreciated the statement of acknowledging I was having a difficult time but on the other hand no matter how this woman had reacted in life she did not have a point of reference to how I felt because I didn't have a point of reference to how I felt. What was meant to be a very simple and straightforward statement threw me into turmoil for a few minutes until I could pull myself together.

Later I considered this for some time and considered how improper that statement is and how much I wished that someone really did understand how I felt so they could explain it to me. It was not until years later that I came to terms with the complexities of the situation. Before that time, I only knew that I was feeling a lot and I would never be able to close all of the things I wanted to say and do with my father. I came to terms with the fact that no one could really know how I was feeling.

Are you ok?

It's OK.

You know people say that all the time. If you want to do something funny take a few minutes and look up what the real story about "OK" is. You will find several answers and as you do consider what it means to ask someone if they are "OK". We have defined "OK" as being normal or being without issue. When we ask if someone is "OK" what we're really asking is, are they normal. This is just like asking someone grieving "how are you doing". It is a superficial question which usually receives a quick and easy response, "I'm ok" or "just taking one day at a time". Asking them if they are "OK" might give them the feeling that you really want to know or that you are interested in their actual feelings.

If someone has just experienced a significant loss, we really need to consider how we are going to help. If we ask a question like "how are you?" or "are you OK?" we are ignoring what is going on at that moment because quite honestly at that moment the answer is right, there in front of you. No, they are not "OK". It will not give them any solace for you to ask the question again. It will not give them any peace of mind to know that you are checking on them again. Instead, it may just add another question that they are already asking themselves.

As we've been pointing out over and over, you will be able to evaluate the situation when you're in front of the person grieving. If a grieving person is in front of you, I can surely say they are not "OK". You also might need to reword your question if you truly want some insight on how the person is doing. Maybe rewording your question or statement will allow those that are grieving to give you an actual answer that is insightful. Try "I know you are not ok, but I wanted to see how you were feeling today or how you are feeling at the moment" or "I wish I had the right words to say" or "I am here for you and I love you" or even "I can't imagine what you are going through or how you feel". Then pause and allow them to tell you, if they choose to, how they feel. It gives those that are grieving an open door to share with you how they are really feeling.

It also so conveys to them that you really are interested in how they are doing at that moment in time.

I'm OK:

We found ourselves in deep grief each and every day since the accident. Though many people want to say something, it is usually "how are you" or "are you doing OK". It's just the normal thing to say, but the answer for a long time will be "no, we are not OK, and we aren't doing well." I could have said "we are doing ok" and waited for them to say "No, you are not" but the entire conversation could be skipped since the answer was self-evident. Often these questions were met by silence.

As I think of the hundreds of conversations that I have had with people since our tragedy, I continued to be asked that same question "how are you doing?" Then the person asking often said "I know you are not ok, so forgive me for asking". This might have been the perfect place to just say "I know your days are tough and I just wanted to check on you to see what I can do to help".

Instead of doing the small talk "how are you?" or "are you ok?" If I could give any advice to anyone it would be to be present in the conversation and maybe not ask questions to the grieving.

I met a lady last week that had lost her son to a tragic accident less than a year ago. She and I spoke about this and how you get a lot of the small talk questions. She told me that she got so tired of being asked "how are you doing?" that she just started responding "I'm ok" to all of them. It appeared she felt that the questions weren't really questions that they wanted to talk about. Did they really want to know how she felt? Were they just asking out of courtesy? It felt to her more like they were just sending a message to touch base and going on with their busy lives.

I honestly believe that some people want to know if you are coping or are you barely getting by? Are sad and crying or are you having a decent day? What I am learning is, it's all in how you ask the question.

Throughout this process I have learned to be very direct with my feelings and when you ask how I am I will be very honest, and you may get more than you bargained for at any time. It is normal for me to say, "Not very good right now" or "It has been a hard day."

One of my daughter's best friends is clearly heartbroken as well. She and her family check in with us about once a week, sometimes more. I feel certain that she really wants to know how we are doing because of what she says to us. She always tells us that she is thinking and praying for us and then she always asks us "what can I pray for today" or "what do you need today that I can pray for". She usually gets a response from us that tells her exactly where we are today and what she can pray for. She then can tell how we are doing for the day or sometime the week and she knows what we need at that time. This helps.

I have a former boss who also has been contacting me since the day of the accident. He never says to me "how are you doing?" he usually states the facts "I have been thinking of you and your family today, I saw something that reminded me of you and started praying for your family". He then proceeds to tell me that he is a great listener, and he is available to talk at any time. When I respond to him, I tell him exactly where we are that day and that week. I do not sugar coat anything. If you are contacting me to check in, I am going to give you the exact place we are at that moment. What I love is his response which is "Thank you for being honest and not just telling me you are fine".

Though I have said this many of times, it's depressing to contact me most of the time because I don't ever say "I am fine" because I am not fine. I am honest and share exactly where I am. I recommend when contacting a grieving person, ask them questions that allow them to tell you exactly how they are feeling. They might not give you all the details but if that makes them feel better to talk about it, you have given them that opportunity. Also share things with them that will be comforting. Knowing they are being thought of or prayed for is comforting and is what they need to know. Having friends, coworkers or former coworkers, high school friends, and family staying in contact with you and genuinely caring about where you are each day or week, makes a difference. I continue to get messages from friends truly checking in on us. Wanting to know where we are at the moment. I remember getting one when things were starting get a little quiet that said, "We are here for you and we have not forgotten." That said it all.

You are Strong

Strong is a word that people like to share with others that are hurting or grieving to try to convince them they are capable of dealing with whatever they are grieving about or whatever is hurting them. It's a way to try and build someone up that appears to be falling apart at the seams. Sometimes what looks like strength is actually shock. In some cases what appears to be strength really isn't. Some people say this about people that have been in extraordinarily strong roles or have been through a lot and they seem to them as strong people.

When you tell someone, they are being strong you might be setting expectations that could be hard to meet by the grieving person. Sometimes those expectations are something the grieving person just might not want to or can't be right now. Sometimes people state that a grieving person is strong, when in fact the one saying it might just want to see them as strong. It's like using reverse psychology on the griever. It's like you might be trying to convince them they are strong to help them be strong.

In many cases it is again someone trying to fix something that is not fixable. It might be a fact that the person struggling, or grieving has been strong all their life. Maybe they have had to take on more than one person should have to, in a lifetime. We both have had our tough times in life. We have seen a family dynamic self-destructed right in front of our eyes. We have seen our stability crumble into nothing. We have had to fight our way to be successful adults by finding our inner drive. We have had to work harder and, in the process, created a different life than most anyone would have expected. We had to be strong for each other and for ourselves. But when people told us this time "You are so strong" or "You're the strongest person I know", it wasn't true because we weren't strong, we didn't want to be strong, and no one was going to convince us otherwise. This was maybe the weakest we had ever been at the same time.

Coaching:

I have been a college coach for half of my adult life, and I know what it looks like to be strong. You have no choice. You had to be strong for the young adults that were facing their own trials and tribulations. Maybe it was my inner core that made me strong even when I was scared or maybe it was a learned behavior and an acceptable persona that I wanted to have to show my kids what it was like to be strong.

This time I didn't want to be strong. I remember hearing people tell me throughout the days following the accident "Pam you are so strong" or "You are the strongest person I know". I didn't want to be strong. If this is what strong looks like and takes on, I didn't want to be strong, not even for a millisecond. All my life I have had to be strong and this time I just didn't want to be strong. I knew I was weak, and I also knew that being strong meant I needed to hold it together, move forward, keep going, and I just didn't want too. I did not have it in me to be strong.

I appreciate that people think that about me but to be honest, this time I didn't want to hear how strong I was, I just didn't want to be in this situation; the darkest place I had ever been. I didn't want anyone to think I was strong enough to handle this type of grief. I just wanted to be freed from the pain I was feeling. I didn't want people to think I was strong enough to handle this, not because I was looking for sympathy, but because I needed those that loved me to see this time, I just couldn't be strong.

I wasn't strong, we weren't strong.

You'll find a way

Each and every day we are faced with the directions we must take. Often, we are challenged with incredible obstacles and near insurmountable tasks.

When it comes to grief the challenges are honestly incredible and potentially near impossible. As we are considering the people that we are about to walk up to and talk to we really need to consider the path we're taking. If you think about it many of us are trying to determine a way to talk to someone who has potentially lost their way. We're going to try to comfort someone who potentially can see no easy path to success or to even feeling better, maybe ever.

Let's stop right there for a second and think about what we're about to do. We wanted to help that person along and at the same time offer them some type of comfort. We have a significant arsenal of words but we're not sure which ones to use. As we step up to the plate getting ready to talk, making a statement like "you'll find a way" may seem self-evident. It's obvious that if this person is going to succeed at anything, they're going to have to "find a way". This is where we have to say over and over to determine where that person is in the grieving process and exactly what they're going through. They may not have a clue of how they're going to "find a way" and if you came to us in the depths of grief and said, "you'll find a way" our first question would be "oh really, just what way is that?"

I know that seems almost confrontational, but we'll all "find a way" and it may be good or it may be bad, but we will "find a way". The solution that is far easier is to take a moment and just offer help. We can't necessarily say that anyone will "find their way", but we can be there with them if they need us. We can walk alongside them as they find their way. Maybe we can even hold a flashlight as we "find a way".

Trying:

Participating in a visitation where hundreds of people are coming to see you, hug you, cry with you, and offer their condolences, is quite a task. It is so soon after you have had to endure the unthinkable. You mentally are having a hard time just focusing on the person standing in front of you. It is such a beautiful time for those that love you and want to share but it's also brutal to be standing for hours and greeting all those people when you are not even sure how you can take the next breath.

Like we have discussed throughout this book, people say things they think will help you, fix it, or even take a little bit of your pain away. They mean well.

As we stood for hours, thanking hundreds of people for coming to pay their respects, I remember a person standing in front of me who was not sure what to say. Eventually they decided that saying "you'll find a way to make it through" was their choice. My thought at the time was, "I really don't have a choice right now, so yes, I will find a way" but what I knew was, it wasn't going to be easy.

As I thought about the phrase "you'll find away", I wondered if that was something that would really help those grieving? The truth be known, "finding a way" is going to happen even if I am not looking for it. Every day since the accident, I am trying to "find a way": a way to put one foot in front of the other; to get out of bed; to be productive each day; and to just deal with each day as it comes. I am "finding a way" but it's one of those things that was said to me that really didn't help at all.

If she could be here still, she would be

Sometimes grief is for good reasons. Often the most difficult grief is for death. We are struggling a little bit writing this as we are trying to keep a more positive tone and be as direct as possible. When somebody is facing that ultimate physical loss of a person there is virtually no easy way to console them. Sometimes the spiritual availability of a person may allow some comfort. It is not up to anyone on the outside to suggest one way or another that there is spiritual comfort, that is up to each individual.

Along that same line, suggesting any type of return or hypothetical situation can be particularly painful. Saying that anyone "would be here if they could be" or stating "they didn't want to go" does not have a positive effect at all. In fact, after thinking about it as we were writing this statement there's virtually no way it will have a positive effect. We discussed this for more than a moment. There are times that we need to take a higher path, and this is one of them. If you get anything out of this book or any of these short chapters, it should be that you need to assess the situation and determine what you should say. Sometimes what you should say is very little, other times what you should say is nothing.

No matter how you approach it, telling someone that their loved one would be there if they could be is just not the right approach. Set it aside and choose another path, please.

Listening:
Over the years I have found the world to be a series of complexities that can only be resolved by an open mind and an open ear. When my sister lost her daughter, I was immediately in a car driving a long distance to be there, no matter what. I was sure there were going to be hundreds of people available as she is very social and very talkative to everyone. She had friends to spare, and I knew many of them would do everything they could to help make her days a little brighter. My reason for being there was to be a buffer if necessary, a listener if necessary, and to do what needed to be done whenever I found it.

From the moment I arrived the house was full of people. Some were very engaged, and some were not so engaged and instead sat closely and listened, only interjecting when necessary.

On the second day I was there, I was listening and talking as needed and I heard someone say, "you know they would be here if they could be". I'm not sure that my sister heard it, nor did I hear them repeat it except for a statement to someone else stating that "no one wants to go they just go when they're called".

I thought about these statements for a considerable time. On one hand they make perfect sense to someone who isn't experiencing grief. I seriously doubt there is anyone in the world that would not stay a little longer if given a choice. I also know that if someone could be there to comfort their loved ones, they definitely would be but then the reasonable side of me took control and I realized that the entire statement was a giant "what if".

Don't get me wrong, "what if" statements are very important in the world and allow for personal growth and a variety of solutions that most people don't think about. In this case, I hoped my sister didn't hear and hoped that if she did, she would quickly forget about this rather insensitive "what if".

This is your new reality

Every day we are faced with the reality of the day before. Reality is a state of things as they actually exist, as opposed to an idealistic idea of them. When people are grieving it is intensified by the facts and the reality of the situation. When someone is taken from earth, those that are left here are the ones that are facing the harsh reality every day. It is not something that you forget when you go to sleep, or don't remember when you wake in the morning. This is not something that most people like to face but you don't get to choose. The saying "it is what it is" is posted in the Urban dictionary and is a phrase that actually means "reality". It is a phrase that seems to simply state the obvious but actually means "it's not going to change". What it really states is "This is *the* reality". When people are grieving it is hard enough to face the day, you don't need others to confirm with you that you now have a new reality. It's obvious. Those that are grieving know the reality, they might not want to face it, but they know it all too well. People do not need to be reminded.

Vivid Statements:

I remember vividly people saying to me multiple times "you are facing your new reality". It was basically reminding me that something would be missing from my family and I would need to be able to face and, for lack of a better word, accept it.

One day my husband had come home after a workout. He was trying to exert a little energy to remove some bad stress that his body was harboring while grieving. As he stood in the gym area an acquaintance of ours came to talk with him. While asking him how we were all doing she proceeded to mention to him that she understood we were getting used to our "New Reality". My husband who doesn't let a lot of things bother him, remembers feeling like he had been smacked in the face. Yes, he was fully aware that our family dynamic had changed and that what we knew in the past, was now gone. It was a new reality for us, one that we didn't ever want to face, but we had no choice. There is no one that needs to be reminded of that. It's hard enough to know that everything you have known has now changed and what you are facing while grieving is something you didn't ask for, nor want. Facing the reality or the new reality is hard for us and for people that are grieving. Be considerate when sharing your feelings about the "new normal" for those that are grieving. Maybe just not saying anything at all would be better than reminding them that their lives have changed forever. There new reality was something they didn't ask for, didn't want, and sure didn't need to be reminded of.

Part 2: The Positives

The way that we approached this book was kind of tricky. Before putting out a list of positive things that you should say or do, we focused on a few negatives. The reason we did it this way was to get people ready to realize the positives and negatives can appear and disappear based on people. What we mean by that is that one person's positive could be another person's negative which we have said before.

It is important as we navigate this book to realize that the only rule, when in the presence of someone who is grieving, is in fact there are no rules. Situations may change and through the course of a few hours, a few days, or even a few months, things may be taken differently and out of context. Take a deep breath, the things that we're going to give you as great positives may be taken as the most amazing positive by some and taken differently by others. It is all based on their past and their needs. These were things that helped us. They were things that made a difference and our hope is they will help you as well.

A Meal Train

No, we are not talking about a big engine running around the country on tracks. A Meal Train is a series of meals that are set up by either someone who coordinates the train or yes, you guessed it, there is an app for that. Imagine having so many people that want to help out a grieving person and imagine that they could be focused together to handle the basic needs, like eating, for an extended amount of time. This takes stress off the person or family that is grieving and allows them to focus on their grieving process.

With a Meal Train you can spread out meals for days, weeks, or longer and in the process allow people to help while also doing good. It also eliminates the one thing that people do not think about in the process, excess waste. The meals in a meal train can be timed to come at the right time and ensure that the person or family is taken care of each day.

If you look up Meal Trains, it will note that they are usually set up for people going through challenging times and it ensures that your loved ones are fed during their difficult times.

Working with other people who want to help for an extended amount of time alleviates a great deal of pressure from the grieving family or friends. This works perfectly 99% of the time but if someone uses cooking to calm their minds, they might not want a Meal Train or food for an extended period. (Yes, there are people out there that still cook and enjoy cooking). Check with the grieving family or close relatives to be sure. In the end, you can create a schedule that works just by keeping the lines of communication open.

All you need to do now is help them eat.

Day One:

People were coming in droves the first morning with breakfast foods, coffee, and drinks, for those that would fill the house with love and support. It was a great way to help us quickly and was greatly appreciated. It took the burden of "feeding an army" off our plate.

One of the greatest things we were offered during our grieving process was a Meal Train. Quite honestly, on the first day the kitchen was at capacity. I remember a dear friend announcing she would be starting a Meal Train so that all this food coming in could be spread out and not go to waste. She saw the need for setting up a meal train very early and began the work to get it all set up. She then posted on social media for people to participate. What we found was that people wanted to help and this was a great way to allow people to help for weeks and in our case months. It allowed those that did not know what to do, but wanted to do something, the chance to provide a meal help throughout the grieving journey. It has been one of the things that continued to remind us daily of those that loved us, supported us, and wanted to help us. Even now, the meal train has ended but we still get people providing meals on occasion which warms our heart and helps us.

The best advice we were given the first week, when people were doing so much and setting up the meals each day, was to allow people to help us. We are a "doing" family. We aren't a family that would ask for help very often but we realized this was a time we needed it. Allowing people to set up and participate in the Meal Train removed the stress of cooking each night for our family. It allowed us extra time to just be together for dinner where we needed to be. Our time was not spent worrying about what we would be cooking or ordering for dinner.

Maybe there is someone out there that would feel that this gesture would indicate they were not capable of taking care of their family or they were unorganized, but I would say to them, enjoy this amazing act of kindness and allow people to help you with meals. It was quite the stress reliever for our family and took a lot of pressure off us.

Recipe cards

One of the greatest gifts during the grieving process was the food that was brought to the house. The meal train had provided us with a monthly schedule of people providing dinner each evening. This was certainly helpful and removed the stress of "what's for dinner" for all of us that were grieving so heavily. Think about what stresses people during a work week and one of the top complaints is figuring out what you are making for dinner or what your family is eating for dinner. When a meal or multiple meals are provided for you, it truly relieves a little stress, no matter what the circumstances are at the time. In comparison, as meals are provided when people are grieving, it not only removes some stress but also allows the family to appreciate all that is being done for them. What is even better than a good home cooked meal that could have been a family favorite or something that is easy to cook and reheat, is a meal with a recipe card attached. If it is a family favorite of the provider, it could possibly be a family favorite of those that are grieving. Attaching a recipe card is a nice touch to a wonderful meal.

One of the things we experienced early on was a meal that arrived one evening from someone we did not even know well. They wanted to help. When they delivered the meal, they also included recipe cards for the meal. It was such a great idea and was we were so appreciative. Other meals were amazing, and I remember my family saying, I wish we knew how to make this. The recipe card was a nice addition to the delicious meal and having the recipe was very appreciated so that when we were ready, we could make it ourselves. Consider including your recipe for your meal if you deliver one. It may just become one of their favorites.

Yummy:
They were bringing enough food for all that were staying here at the time. When my family members were here to help, the meal train provided enough for everyone. When everyone went home and it was just us, the meal train was reduced to be fitting for a smaller number of portions.

Some of the meals that were brought to us included recipe cards. Some did not. I remember during the process when someone had dropped off a meal and we had enjoyed the flavorful dinner, my son asked me if I knew how to make this particular chicken and rice dinner. The meal was so delicious, and we all loved it, but I had never made it before.

I could have easily looked up a recipe on the internet to find what was needed to make a similar meal, but it might not have been the exact same. It would have been better if the meal had a recipe already attached to it. It would be easier to have the person providing it to share their recipe for their meal. We would have had over 40-60 new recipes if everyone would have shared the recipes for each meal.

Another great reason to include the recipe is to see the ingredients for the items you have supplied. With food allergies at an all-time high, people know what is in a meal so they can decide to have it based on their allergies. Including a recipe is a nice gesture and, in most cases, will be appreciated for years to come. To be quite honest, I didn't really think of this until someone dropped off a meal one evening and inside the basket of food were recipes for the meal provided and the cookies, they also included for dessert. It dawned on me then, everyone should include a recipe for the meals they provide. That way they not only know the ingredients, but they also have the recipe to enjoy forever.

Be There:

An important part of the grieving process is to walk the journey alongside those that are grieving. Whether you drive five minutes down the street or fly sixteen hours to be there, it will mean the same. Being there means you love them and want to support them through the grieving process. Though it might not seem to you that it will make a difference, I promise you, it does.

Some people will come the first day and you might not see them again. Some people will come and see all the other people there and decide that they are not needed, but they are. Some will wait to come when the crowd of people dies down, and they will be needed to walk the journey when the crowd has gone back to their normal everyday life.

All these people are needed, the ones at the beginning and the ones that will walk the long journey. Of course, there are those that will do both or won't do either. The important thing to those that are grieving is, they are not walking this alone. There is no confusion in the statement, only some strong enlightenment.

Being there is one of the most important things that can happen. As you find a way, you might find that your presence is appreciated far more than you're being shown or that you feel. Most people think they are just one of the many that are coming, and they aren't needed or even significant. As you work through it, you may suddenly realize how important a simple moment can be.

We have to say whole heartedly that when you visit the house of those grieving or a memorial service you may be paying respect to the person who has left the earth, but you are there for the people who are alive. The expectation is quite definitively that we should support each other in our lives no matter what. We can rationalize quite easily 100 different reasons to not be at someone house who is grieving, a memorial service, or a Celebration of Life. When we do so, self-preservation and fear can be at the top of the list even when you consider the fear was not knowing what to say or knowing what to do. Sometimes distance can be a factor, but you have to ask yourself, is it really? Ask yourself honestly would this person be there for you and then figure out whether you should show up.

As you walk through this section of the book keep in mind that every person is different and that sometimes just being there is enough. Also, as you read through this section of the book remember that when thinking about these positives don't use them as definitive statements. Saying things like "you will" or "you should" with just about anything can be taken wrong. As we walk through this valley of positive items and parables you really do need to put them in your own words.

Take your time read through and know there won't be a test at the end but maybe there should be.

First Weeks:
Though many of the first weeks are a blur to me. I remember thinking throughout the process about the people that I saw coming in the door. They were bringing food, sharing hugs, and sitting all around our house just trying to take a small portion of the pain away. We were suffering but it helped. There is something about seeing those faces that have made a small dent in this thing called life.

Walking into our house to share in our pain could not have been fun. Believe me it's something that grieving people need. We needed to know that people were walking alongside of us, supporting us, and that they were willing to walk this entire difficult journey with us. What we were faced with during the first few weeks was the feeling of being alone. This was a feeling no one could easily understand. It's scary to be in an unknown set of circumstances that you never expected to experience. The thought of doing that without family and friends was just scary.

If I could give any advice about being there or not being there, it would be to BE THERE. Don't ask if they need you, they do. It is really hard for grieving people to ask for help or ask to not be alone. Our lives are already in such turmoil that we don't want to ask anyone for anything. Sometimes we just want to sit and grieve. We probably should do that while we have people with us. Yes, the tears were uncontrollable and the pain we were experiencing was unbearable at times, but we still needed people to be there with us.

I know for me and my family, we needed every single person that showed up, no matter what they did or did not say or do, we needed them. Each person brought their own love and support to the table, which we needed. We are not ashamed to say we still need people. We still need those type of people in our lives that are going to walk this very long journey with us.

Now, looking back, being there meant we had people holding us up when we were just so heartbroken and terribly sad.

People came:
We can't even express on paper what "being there" really meant to our family. It actually still means a lot to all of us. The amount of family and friends that traveled hours to get to us the first few days and the many days following, just to be there, will never be forgotten. These people left their own responsibilities to be there with us, day in and day out. How can we truly say, "Thank you"?

The amount of people that wanted to be there to support us during the mid-day service and left their everyday lives to spend the day honoring our sweet daughter will always be appreciated. There were so many people that were "there". Some people were there in person, and some were on the phone. Everyone was making sure we were doing the best that we could. They were amazing people. They were "there".

Being "there" doesn't mean just when the grieving starts. It is way more than just that. Being there means you have made eye contact, shared a hug, made the phone call, sent the message, maybe even multiple times. Being there is so important but is one of the hardest things for people to do because most people don't know what to do. Being there can be a very intimidating experience if you haven't been in that situation before or you feel inadequate in the grieving department. However, being there for support and comfort is a key component during the grieving process.

Families like ours still need people to be there. We needed them then and we still need them now. We are approached by people all the time that have said to us, "We didn't come by because we didn't want to bother you", or "We weren't there because we knew you had tons of people there with you".

I often wish they had just come.

Weeks Later:

I remember three weeks after our daughter went to Heaven, I had a birthday. It was so irrelevant at the time and seemed like something that I would have rather skipped over this year. I didn't care about my birthday, or for that matter, I didn't care if anyone even knew it was my birthday. My birthday falls a few days before Christmas. All my life it has always been a busy time for people. It is a beautiful time of the year, but a very busy time. This year I didn't care about any of it. I remember my sweet niece and nephew coming up from Alabama that day to not celebrate. They knew it would not be a fun day for me, so they decided to be there to walk this "not so fun day" with me. They just wanted to be there. They gave me options to go out, to stay in, to sit and do nothing, or find something to preoccupy my mind. What they were really saying to me was "We are here to carry the burden for you today. You don't have to carry it alone especially on your birthday." They had prepared themselves to know that this might not be a fun day. Still, they were not going to allow me to face it alone or without them. They had no expectations for the day, just to walk along side of me and carry some of the weight.

That evening I was sitting in my kitchen, just trying to get through the day without really having to think about my birthday. I heard a knock at the door. As I walked into our foyer, I saw one of my dearest friends and her family standing on my porch. They had again made the 4-hour drive from

Georgia, after making it 3 other times in three weeks, to now acknowledge my birthday. They too knew it wouldn't be a celebration at all, but instead they wanted to be there for me. This was one of the things for which I will never be able to express my gratitude. It meant a great deal to me.

Both my family and my friends came that day to see me because they knew I needed them, they knew I would be feeling a range of emotions and they wanted to be there to help me handle them, to cope with them, and to get through the day.

Sometimes during the grieving process there are a lot of people that are there at the beginning but as time goes by, people go back to their normal lives, and it leaves you to take on each day by yourself. I have had girl friends that have made it a point to spend time with me every week, to not only check on me, but to be there. Talking is good and having people be there is even better. This same thing goes for my husband and kids. They need friends to walk the Journey with them. No matter what relationship you have with those that are grieving, you have a place.

I'm going:
Those that know me well know that I have never been good with people grieving and quite honestly, I just didn't know what to say or do myself. In most cases, I tried to avoid at all costs going into a situation where the people around me were in deep grief and never knew what to say.

A few weeks after my daughter's accident one of my dear friends came over to spend a few hours with me. We have been friends for many years and watched our youngest daughters grow up during the same time. She decided to share a story with me about not knowing what to do. She had been at one of her friends' houses as the morning news was sharing the story of our tragedy. She went into shock hearing the news and said to her friend, "what should I do?" Her friend responded with no questions "GO THERE." She left her friend's house to get into her car where she called her husband and shared the news she had just learned. He said to her "you have to go there, now." She told me that her own insecurities on how to handle these situations almost forced her to not come to my house. She said when she drove up there were so many cars that she was more than a little intimidated. Still the burning need to come in and support me was bigger than her fears.

I would guess she felt like many others, I am sure of it. It's the not knowing what to do and feeling that you won't do or say the right things that hinder you from doing what the grieving person really needs. The advice and encouragement from her friend and husband were exactly what we want to encourage those reading this book to do, GO THERE. You will not regret it. When you arrive, you will know if your stay needs to be short or if you might need to stay for hours. You will know. Don't pass up the opportunity to allow those grieving to feel your support. It's much needed.

I remember she came that day and has continued to see me every week. She truly defines what it is to "be there."

Send texts and emails

Electronic communication has changed the world. We can now get in touch with each other very rapidly and we can relate thoughts and ideas in a matter of moments. Unfortunately, this is sometimes coupled with an expectation that people reply instantly. There is a skit that goes around as well as many stories and short videos where someone's phone doesn't work correctly after a text is sent and people become emotionally charged by it to the point of going nearly crazy. After you have decided what you want to say to someone who is grieving or even before, you should always add a nice little note saying, "please don't feel you have to respond" or "I don't expect a response." If you say it, make sure you don't expect it.

This does two things for those grieving. First and foremost, it sets an expectation that those that are grieving should not feel any pressure to try and respond. It also allows the person that sent the messages the freedom to not be waiting for a response. The recipient is not obligated to send a response now, later, or even ever.

With most people I can say wholeheartedly they will get to it. It may not be today or tomorrow or even next week but sometimes the emotional toll on a person during the first few weeks or months may cause them to avoid interaction simply because it adds difficulty. This doesn't mean you are being difficult or everything that you're doing isn't appreciated but instead it means that they need time to think through all the things that they're going through and feeling at the time.

Adding that one little line to a text or email will quiet a great deal of angst. Of course, if they have set their phone aside or given it to someone else to handle during this time. They will be thankful there was no expectation when they finally begin to answer.

Pings:
I remember the first 10 hours after the accident and how many texts, emails, calls, and messages that were coming in. I also remember the "pings" from the notifications on my social media, coming in. This meant

that my account was being tagged or people were sending direct messages from social media. The feeling was overwhelming, and we were just at the tip of processing what just happened to our family and what our lives would look like in the future. It was heartbreaking to know that everyone was hearing the news and we just did not have it in us to respond.

I do remember the nights were so long and dark and I would sit up at night and read all the messages that people had sent me. The pain was so deep that I cried through most of them, and I couldn't respond to a great deal of them, but I did read them. Even in my darkest hours, I appreciated those messages.

Social media is a computer-based technology that allows people to share ideas, information, news, thoughts and to contact other people. I personally could not go on social media after our daughter's accident. I knew it would be filled up with pictures and stories that my heart just could not bear to read or see right then. I knew it would be too much for me to handle, it was too soon for me. From experience, I knew there would be a lot of amazing posts about her.

Other moms that were also walking this same journey have told me they received a lot of comfort when reading all the messages on social media. I personally think it depends on your circumstances and the person grieving. Everyone is different. What I do know is the people that took the time to write to me or send me messages had my best interest at heart. They genuinely wanted to communicate with me, and at this time, it was the best way to do that.

When sending emails, you have a much wider range, and it gives the grieving person an opportunity to read it more effectively later. Most people have gotten into the habit of reading text messages, emails, social media messages, and all the other electronic communication methods on their cell phone. Still having the ability to read it on a computer even through potentially teary eyes, is an advantage. It provides a little protection to the grieving as many people do not have their email notifications turned on. As we saw in our circumstances, the text message notifications were constant during this different and challenging time.

With that in mind consider email or even a nicely worded letter over text messages unless you are a close family member. I have seen a grieving person up close with their phone vibrating faster than a busted chainsaw with all of the people sending their concerns. It is overwhelming to say the least, but the communication is needed. It accurately shows those that are grieving they are being thought about, prayed for, and sent beautiful messages, stories and memories. I personally print these emails after I read them. I want to keep them to read forever.

I know another mother that was in deep grief a few years ago. She and I were talking about this book we were writing and how we wanted to help people know what to do or say to people that are grieving. She proceeded to tell me that while we were discussing this, she went back in to re-read messages that were sent to her years ago. After reading those messages years later, she decided to respond to some of those messages she never responded to during the unthinkable time. She said it warmed her heart to go back and re-read these precious messages that were sent to her. She mentioned that as she read them, she realized that there were so many "great" ones that were sent. A few years ago, she wasn't able to appreciate the heart felt messages, words of encouragement, prayers, and thoughts. Now, a few years later, she could. She will forever grieve the loss of her son, but she had a newfound appreciation for the loved ones that sent these letters and messages during that time in her life that she could only be physically present for before.

My suggestion is, if you think you should text them, email them, call them, leave a message for them, or send them a social media message, YOU SHOULD. It will make a difference even years later. Don't let your own self-doubt stop you because you don't know what to write or you don't want to bother them. It will mean a lot that you did send the messages or made the calls for years to come.

I know in this new age many people prefer electronic communication over in person or phone communication. Phone communication during these types of situations might be difficult or impossible. Text and email and other written methods are quite common and might be easier to deliver. Still, making sure the person grieving knows you do not expect a response now or maybe ever is necessary and is an incredibly positive gesture. I know it helped me.

The calls:

I remember not being able to sleep much at all during the first few months. I would go to sleep but wake during the early morning hours to a very dark reality. A reality that encapsulated a circle of questions, worries, and thoughts that would not allow my mind to shut down. I would get out my phone and read all the messages that were sent to me that day. I remember thinking how peaceful it was to get messages that didn't expect a response, they were just telling me they were lifting us up in prayer or we were in their thoughts daily. Some would share a sweet story about Haley Sue that we hadn't heard or remembered. There was a sense of calmness that was attached to these messages that at the time I didn't appreciate. As I look back and remember now, I can feel some of the comfort those messages brought me. I go back and read them during the late-night hours still.

I still have every single one of those messages on my phone, in my email, on my social media and I never plan to remove them.

Those people that sent them were like angels watching over me when I couldn't sleep a wink. As hard as the nights were, when things are quiet and calm, the notifications, Bible verses, prayers, and the sweet messages were what kept me going.

Help

This will be a little different. According to the Merriam Webster dictionary, the definition of help is "to make it easier for someone to do something by offering one's services or resources". Help can come in so many forms and fashions.

We could pretty easily have named the entire book "Help! The positives and negatives you can do for the grieving." That name seemed a little direct, so we took a little bit lighter approach. We can define help ourselves by how we perceive help. There are little things and big things that we often do not consider because we haven't experienced everything yet nor will we ever experience "everything". We must remember that when we walk into a situation where people are grieving the help, they need maybe different than the help you would need. This means listening or paying attention and then making decisions on how you want to help is key.

The amount of help you want to give depends completely on the amount of help you can give. Some people will be there constantly and will want to help by giving of themselves and their time. Some people may be more passive, and their help may be in the form of plants, food, money, cleaning, and a score of other things that we will outline as this chapter progresses. We will also have listed a couple of extra credit ideas that came up in our situations and that are really cool. The end game is to make certain that whatever you do to help makes a difference and doesn't necessarily require you to be thanked at that moment or maybe ever.

In the complete chaos that surrounds the grieving, there could be a considerable number of things overlooked that were incredibly meaningful. If they aren't overlooked, it might just be so overwhelming to try and thank all those people who are doing so much. Help comes in all shapes and sizes when people are grieving, and their lives have been turned upside down. If you are giving the help, you are trying to think of way to make their lives a little better, for even a moment. If you are the one grieving, you might not know what to do or even say to all the people that are helping. It's overwhelming at times.

We grew up in an age and time when you wrote Thank You notes to everyone for everything. You never missed a Christmas, birthday, or specially occasion where you received help or a gift that you didn't hand write a Thank You note, add a stamp, and mail it. When people that grew up like that are faced with situations where people are helping so much, they might start to feel overwhelmed with thoughts like "how can I ever thank everyone for all that they are doing"? It might sound silly to some, but based on the way we were raised, some might feel the need to start writing 100's of Thank You notes.

This is where some great advice comes in, you don't have to write anything. You can thank people as they stand in front of you, or you can thank people on social media as a group. You do not have to write Thank You notes to every single person who reached out to you. These people that have come to help shouldn't expect acknowledgement and probably don't expect a Thank You. They understand.

Help is such a difficult thing to define when trying to help those that are grieving. It requires significant listening skills and the ability to grasp the needs of the person you are talking to. We forget that sometimes and instead of looking at their needs we focus on what we think they need. This doesn't always work very well. There are things that you might just know they need, such as a hug, or tissue, or a glass of water. Sometimes what they really need is a listening ear. Through you listening to them you will hear things that they might really need. For instance, you might be talking to them, and you hear them say, "I forgot to pick up my medicine at the pharmacy." That is your key to get in your car and go to the pharmacy and pick this up for them.

For those helping, allow yourself to help but don't expect anything in return.

Trying to help:

Quite some time ago one of my best friends lost his mother. She was a very nice person but also was somewhat of a hermit. She stayed in her own place and did not interact heavily with others except through the Internet. My friend kept in touch with his mother through the Internet constantly and as she got ill, he got more and more involved to the point of finally bringing her to his home to stay.

The end was sad as she was constantly upset about how she was taken away from her home even though she was no longer able to take care of herself. I was initially concerned about her situation but during her time at his home she and my friend grew much closer. I think they had a good last few months together. We should all realize how important being together is for people and how it grew their relationship. It's just unfortunate that it was at the end of her life.

I consistently offered to help and was there for both of them as needed. When she passed away, I stepped back for a few moments and just asked what was needed. There wasn't necessarily a lot and sometimes it was just the offer that made the difference. I remember it meaning something that I was there for them. His gratitude towards me was that I would gladly do anything to make certain things were going well for him. As we stood at the gravesite, I was there and let him know whatever he needed from me, I would do.

Isn't this the definition of help? Not just the act of doing something but the willingness to do whatever it takes at any time. In the end, I hope I helped him in every way I could to make his life better during the difficult time he faced.

I don't know how you feel

It's so important to think before you speak not only when dealing with those grieving but in life. As we have explained throughout this book, there are many things that maybe shouldn't be said to people as they are grieving. Some things need to only be said later when the veil of grief isn't so thick. As many things we have noted that didn't help us during the process, there is one that stood out to us that did touch our hearts. It was so true and honest and just made sense. "I don't know how you feel". When people would say this to us, they were saying, "I don't know how bad you are hurting, I don't really know what you are going through, and I have not experienced this same pain before". The pain we felt was heavier than they could even imagine, and they recognized that immediately.

"I don't know how you feel" was acknowledging that we were in great pain and our grief was real. We realize that everyone has grieved in some form or fashion. Everyone has experienced pain whether it was physical pain or emotion pain. Stating that you don't know what someone is going through, or you don't know how someone is able to get up each day, shows that you see the pain and the grief and the struggle we are having as a family. Letting us know you "don't know how we feel" means you are empathizing with us and not trying to compare your pain with our pain or your grief with our grief.

Throughout the grieving process some will have so many people say, "I don't know what you are going through because I have never been in your shoes". It is a definite that the grieving would not want anyone to go through what they are experiencing. In our case it was the hardest thing a parent could ever go through. The grieving will be relieved to know that people are not going to compare stories, or exchange conversation about how things felt compared. People will say just remember saying to her, "it's so painful" and she replied, "I can only imagine". People can only imagine how it feels if they have not felt this level of grief, and even then, that imagination should not be shared.

We can honestly say that if you are mobile and are a reasonable adult you can come up with a multitude of ways to help those that are grieving even if you can't be there the entire time. As you do, you will become part of a solution and a great story that will live on even if it is never told.

Thank you:

During the first couple of weeks after the accident I remember people were in and out of our house daily. They took out the trash often, they cleaned out the refrigerator so it could hold all the food being brought to the house, took care of our dogs, they brought food, they cleaned kitchen and bathrooms, drove people around that needed to get places, sat and talked to people, and so much more. Some people would just come sit with me as I grieved. Some would check on our kids, some would sit with my husband.

One of our closest family friends stayed at the house for a considerable amount of time during the first month. She spent time answering the phone and messages coming in. She paid attention to social media to make certain people were answered when they sent messages. She freed us from responding to all of these communications. She did this so that we weren't constantly overwhelmed by greetings and condolences. She in no way knew how we were feeling, she just knew that there were things that needed to be done and she was going to do them.

Her patient kindness and self-sacrifice will be remembered always. At one point she said she did not know how we were feeling, but she knew she had to be there. It is friends like that that will make you understand how important good people are in your life.

Flowers and the Flower shop

Flowers seem to be the go-to when people are hurting, sick, happy or unhappy, celebrating, showing love, or when people are grieving. It's an American tradition for people to send flowers as respect or sympathy for the bereaved. This custom allows people to express their feelings. It is a beautiful gesture and an easy purchase to show love and support during a tough time. Even when grieving people ask that people send money to a charity of their choice in lieu of flowers, a lot of the time, people still send flowers. It is a scientifically proven fact that flowers have a positive impact on happiness. They brighten a room, and they leave a beautiful fragrance, which can help the mood of those surrounding them.

Sometimes, however, it is overwhelming if you receive multiple bouquet that are sent to you within a short amount of time. When a family is grieving, they really don't get to really appreciate the beauty or the effect of flowers. Sometimes they can't think of anything other than what they are going through and they actually miss the beauty of what has been sent. When there are a lot of flowers that have been sent to one location, usually the house of those grieving, it gets overwhelming. Especially when they are trying to comprehend why they are even in this emotional situation.

If you are trying to decide what to do and you can't be there for someone physically, you don't know what to send, you aren't able to share or send a meal, or you just love flowers and want to send them, consider waiting just a little while before you send flowers. Wait until the madness and commotion have settled down and those that are grieving can appreciate the special nature of your gift. It is a good idea to wait until the ceremony is over and everyone supporting the grieving has gone back to their normal lives. Wait until the ones grieving are transitioning into what their days will look like moving forward. Then send flowers. Send them when they least expect them. That nice surprise will brighten their day and they will actually get to enjoy the aroma of fresh flowers and the beauty of your gift.

When picking out those flowers, think about what would brighten your day if they were sent to you. Would a nice bouquet of flowers of all colors brighten your day, if so, send that type of arrangement? If sending white flowers is what you prefer to send them. It still is the gesture of sending flowers that is really appreciated but when those people are living with the reality of their grief receiving a beautiful bouquet of flowers or a plant a little latter may allow them to enjoy the gift more.

A lot of people will still send flowers for the service or for the home early, and that is ok, just remember that when you chose flowers or plants a great many people will chose the same. Receiving multiple arrangements can become overwhelming and your slightly postponed gift may actually be appreciated more.

One at a time:
The first day after our daughter's accident, the doorbell started ringing incredibly early in the day, a beautiful bouquet was delivered. Shortly after that, another bouquet was delivered, then another and then another and within the first seven days, we have received 43 bouquets of flowers. This was just within the first seven days.

Though they were extremely beautiful, we could not even begin to appreciate them fully because there were so many. They were being delivered when we couldn't even think about how to take our next breath. I remember people answering the door or picking up the spray of flowers from the porch. They would walk around the house trying to find a place to put them and would often set them on the floor temporarily. At one point I remember going out to the den and the ping-pong table had been opened and there were flower arrangements covering every inch of the table. There had been so many that people could not find places to put them, so they put them all on the ping pong table. It was absolutely overwhelming. They were all beautiful, but still overwhelming.

I remember sitting at the kitchen table after about the thirtieth bouquet had been delivered and I thought to myself, "I don't even know who sent all of these". I also thought, "how in the world can I thank everyone for these flowers". I took the time and went around and read all the cards; it was a lot to take in at the time. I remember the smell throughout the house, it smelled just like a florist and was always pleasant. After the 8th day of getting flowers, I remember thinking there must be a better way to do this. I started thinking how this could be better when people are hurting and grieving, and others want to send flowers.

I sat and looked around my house with flowers on every single table, countertop, Ping-Pong table, end table, kitchen table, kitchen counter and more. I considered how nice it would have been if I would have received these flowers arrangements one at a time. Maybe if they arrived every single week for forty-three weeks instead of forty-three bouquets at one time. I remember thinking, maybe they could be have been sent once a month which would mean we would have received fresh flowers for almost four years, based on the amount we received the first eight days. We could have received fresh flowers twice a month for two years or any other combination of time.

Now that was a concept I wish someone would have put into place for us. I knew that this would be a great way to be able to appreciate the wonderful flower arrangements each time they arrived. Receiving them once or twice a month would have allowed us to brighten our home with fresh flowers, enjoy each bouquet as they were delivered, and genuinely appreciate and thank those who sent them. We could have more easily reflected on the relationship we had with every single person that sent these wonderful gifts.

Note to those that own a Floral Shop: I am not a florist however there were only two or three florists in our town that did all the bouquets that were ordered. I wish that they would have noticed they had already delivered multiple arrangements to our house from the first day or two and implemented a better plan for those sending them and those receiving them. It would have been great if the florist could have suggested alternatives to people on the other end of the phone when they were placing their order. They could have relayed that they had already delivered multiple bouquets to the house and suggested a better plan for getting us flowers so that we could actually enjoy them and appreciate them more.

What if when the person who called the florist to send flowers to our home would have been told "We have delivered multiple arrangements to their home already and we suggest that we deliver a card to them that states you have ordered flowers and they will be delivered two weeks from now or in a different month." That way the person sending them still pays the florist, so the florist isn't losing business but what the florist is doing is allowing the recipient to appreciate the flowers and not get overwhelmed by sheer numbers. At the same time, the flowers will be appreciated when things slow down a little. The florist would be able to send fresh flowers in a few weeks when the house is empty, and they will need something to brighten the day.

As the recipient of over forty arrangements of flowers and plants, getting them every couple of weeks would have been a blessing. We would have enjoyed getting the card stating they would be arriving in a few weeks and would have been happy to still know that someone special had sent them and always be looking forward to the magic they give.

As time goes by, you might forget that flowers are coming and what a joy that would be to receive these flowers when there are no other flowers in the house. Receiving them in a few weeks with a new card that says what they wanted it to say, would have been beautiful. We say all of this to say we appreciated and loved every single flower sent or dropped off, but we could have appreciated their beauty and aroma even more had we been able to spread them out a little or even a lot.

Another downfall with getting all the flowers at one time was they all started dying at the same time. Many that are grieving have lost someone or something very special to them. It's a lot to then be surrounded by flowers that are also dying. It can be tough. There were days when I just didn't think I could handle anything else dying. We were a grieving family and now we had forty-three bouquets of flowers dying all over the house. Watching these beautiful flowers, EVERYWHERE, dying amongst us made me think, surely there is a better way to do this for our family or any family that is grieving.

I suggest that before you send a bouquet, just think of the timing. Think about if they will get to appreciate these flowers or are you just sending them to make sure that you do something right now. Maybe you are a "check the box" type of person and you need to do this so that you can mark it off your to do list. Maybe you are a person that needs to send flowers because you received flowers yourself and you knew it brightened your day and you are trying to reciprocate for those grieving. Maybe you are sending these because you were raised and taught to send flowers when someone is grieving and sending them later just doesn't seem appropriate to you. No matter the reason, they will be appreciated, but consider who is going to get to appreciate them or why am I sending these now as opposed to later when they can enjoy their beauty more easily. If you come to the conclusion they must go now, it's ok, but if you can see that sending them later might get a better outcome, I would say wait just a little while.

Empty house:

I remember coming home a few weeks after the accident and finding a bouquet of flowers sent to me from the guys at work. I brought them into the house where now I had no flowers because the initial 43 bouquets had died. I sat them on our kitchen island and was able to really reflect on who sent them, the card they wrote, and where my heart was at this moment. Our house was now empty of family and friends, flowers, and visitors. Receiving this bouquet a little later was such a beautiful thing. I remember thinking how much I loved them because I was now in a place where I could appreciate them a little bit more. My heart wasn't even an ounce healed but the fact that I could actually think about why they were being sent was heartwarming. Even though everyone outside of our home had gone back to their lives, work, and activities, people were still thinking of us, praying for us, and sending us a nice gesture to let us know we were still not alone. It was beautiful. It is also one of the arrangements I remember the most because for about two weeks, it was the only one we had to look at each day.

If you own a flower or Gift Shop, I think people making the purchase would appreciate your insight and help in their purchase and the timing of delivery. They trust that you would put together a beautiful arrangement and I do believe they would trust that you postponing the delivery is a better plan for those receiving them.

Cry Together

There is a sense of appreciation and connection with someone who cries while you are crying. It's a way that we show the person crying that we understand and feel at least some of their pain. There are many people that would say "I'm not a crier" and that's ok.

There is something about someone sharing your grief and heartache the same way that you are outwardly expressing those emotions. This is one of the lessons we learned along the way. As we previously spoke a few chapters before this, crying is good for you. It's a way to express your feelings. Let us reiterate, it's absolutely ok to cry. When you do cry and someone cries with you, it allows you to see that they too are grieving with you.

There were many that grieved with us that never shed a tear in our presence. There were also people that cried right beside us, just as hard as we did. Both were showing us their support. If someone is holding back their tears because they don't want to add to the sorrow the grieving person is feeling, its ok. If someone feels the need to cry and if the time and place is appropriate, they should cry. For those that are grieving, it lets them know that they were not walking this journey alone.

The First Night

A year ago, I would tell you that I am not a crier. I think there are people that just naturally get emotional about things that others don't get as emotional about. 10 years ago, you might find me hugging someone that is crying but it wasn't a natural instinct for me to be crying alongside them. This is not because I didn't feel their pain, but I just didn't cry often. Maybe this is the way we were raised or how we learned to cope but crying just didn't come naturally.

I remember the night of the accident, a few hours after we had arrived home, there was so much chaos going on around us. There were so many emotions happening from everyone in the house. There were calls that I needed to make to family and non-family members. These were the hardest calls I would ever have to make in my lifetime. Each and every call was hard, sharing the tragic news was more than my lips could utter. While making these calls, I remember distinctively the crying that went on, on the other end of the line. These calls went to my family members and friends that had played a very valued part of my adulthood. I remember trying to navigate through that night and through the next morning. It was like walking in quicksand. I was lost. I didn't know what to do. I had lost complete control of what I knew my life to be.

I was trying to put two thoughts together late that evening when I just couldn't function. It was apparent that I needed to talk with people that might help me make sense of any of this situation. Maybe I just needed others to cry along side of me. I remember sending a message to a girlfriend at 3:45 a.m. asking her "are you awake". In 99.9% of cases, my friends would not answer that early in the morning, but this time an answer came. She responded "yes", and minutes later I was on the phone with her trying to get words out of my mouth while sobbing uncontrollably. I recall telling her what had happened and then on the other end of the phone hearing her cry, cry as hard as I was crying. We cried together for hours, we cried until daylight.

I will never forget that call. I will never forget the tears that she shed that morning with me. She was so compassionate, putting her own need of sleep aside so that she could cry with me. She wanted to take just an ounce of my pain away. She wanted to help me.

This was just the beginning of the calls that were made in the night and during the early morning. The next call and the next call to friends and family got the exact same response. So many tears were shed, call after call. Through the tears on the other end, as sad as they were, convinced me I wasn't alone. They meant a lot. The more people I told the more tears that were shared. It sounds a little crazy but there was a sense of comfort when I saw and heard someone sharing our grief. Sharing your tears, sharing your heartache didn't change the outcome, but it did allow us to be assured that we were not alone in all of this.

Elizabethtown:

I had just lost my father and in the whirlwind that followed realized that things were going to be very different for me in my life. It was true that I was an adult, but I had spent a lot of time working to build a relationship with my dad and all that was gone now. The funeral was very different and for the most part was just a memorial service. Well, it was a memorial service that packed a large church with people standing outside. I gave a eulogy that was heartfelt and though I did it easily before the actual ceremony when I was in front of everyone and seeing my father's picture there, I had a difficult time finishing.

So here we were back at home, and I am trying to come to terms with everything I'm experiencing. My wife, who knows me well, decided we should go see a movie and just slow down for a little while. She knows how much I love movies and she picked out one that was local to the Kentucky area that neither of us had seen before. We went to the theater to see the movie "Elizabethtown", bought tickets and sat down.

For those of you that do not know the movie "Elizabethtown" it is about a son who loses his father and realizes all of the idiosyncrasies that he has been missing out on and all of the family and friends that he had set aside for success. The focus is on taking the father's ashes somewhere special and how to do so. There is a good love story mixed into it all but in the end all of that fell away for me.

From about twenty minutes into the movie until about three days after the movie I cried. I cried about the movie, I cried about my dad, I laughed about the choice of a movie, then I cried some more just for the sake of crying.

I will never forget as we walked out of the theater my wife stopping me and holding me for a minute as the tears flowed down my face to my already dampened shirt. Her statement to me was easy and quite accurate, "I guess that wasn't the best choice."

To this day we still laugh about it and at least now I can watch Elizabethtown and not cry the entire time. For me though, crying with her, and with the theater, meant the world to me.

Make Decisions

Dealing with difficult situations is often hard for people. Close friends and even not so close friends struggle often with the idea of what they should do or say. They are going through their own type of grief attempting to determine what their place is and how they need to approach this difficult time. We must be truly clear that not making a decision is a decision within itself.

Sometimes it's ridiculously hard to get across to people how easy it is to make a difference. People look for some grandiose gesture that can change what has happened or suddenly make it right. Sometimes people go even further and try to make certain that they "fix" everything the best that they can and in the process don't really understand what they were addressing.

Take a deep breath. This is going to be really hard to read. You can't fix anything. If you're dealing with a grieving person who has suffered a tremendous loss, there is nothing that you can do or say that is going to change the fact that they are a grieving person and have suffered a tremendous loss. We know this is pretty hard for many people to understand as a significant number of the population will just want to "make it better".

Here's an easy solution:

Instead of trying to come up with the perfect solution, come up with a solution. Instead of trying to come up with the perfect gift, get a gift. Instead of trying to go to the nth degree and say something that truly makes some type of difference, make a difference. I'm sure you're seeing a pattern here.

One of the things that we can say over and over is that there are lots of good things to say and do but you have to make the decision to say or do them. We've given and will continue to give lots of suggestions for things to do that might make the grieving a little better, things to say that might ease something, and things to buy that could be meaningful. A key factor is you and your ability to decide to make things happen. Your decision to act could be the decision that makes a difference.

In a time of grieving many people may be very confused and thinking about a million things at once. We have stated this a few times and we know that during the grieving process they are thinking about a great deal. Making decisions about key elements will be at the forefront of a grieving persons mind, but there are many decisions that just are not at the top of the list. When you are asking the people grieving open ended questions you are basically asking them to make a decision and putting the responsibility of telling you what to do, back on those grieving. As you can imagine, being in this spot is like being out in the ocean, with waves as tall as buildings hitting you, crashing into you, and you feeling like you are being held underwater for longer than you can breathe. Just when you think you won't make it out, you are given a lift up to the surface to then take a breath before the next set of waves come crashing down on you again.

We get it, people just don't want to feel as if they are bothering you. They don't really know what you need, so they just make a vague statement. It could be "let me know if you need anything" or "call me if I can do anything". Those that are grieving are often too preoccupied with dealing with the moment while thinking they don't want to burden anyone else either.

Take your time, listen, and see what needs to be done, then make a decision to do it. You may find that your small decisions made a big difference.

The second we were standing in:
From the moment that we shared our horrific news with very close friends of ours, they made the decision to show up. Our long-time friends came to the house to be with our kids until we got home. We had friends waiting in the neighborhood to come help carry the burden that was about to be unloaded on my family. The youth pastors made the decision to wait in their car and come in when our daughter was told. They were

there to help. It was so important to have these people there to help us carry the burden and help us make the decisions that we might miss. They couldn't change anything, but they made the decision to help us walk this journey.

We had multiple people in and out. We also had those people that decided to show up just to be with us. As uncomfortable as it was for them to come to our house unannounced, they also had to witness all the pain and sorrow we were enduring. It could not have been easy.

Their selfless decisions helped us. We had hundreds of people that sent messages about coming to the house or getting us things that were needed. They looked for us to decide in this overwhelming time. There were so many that didn't ask, they just decided and were there. We were having a hard time even thinking beyond the second we were standing in, so we certainly couldn't think about answering messages about what we needed or if we wanted people there.

What we found was the people that dropped messages to us that said "we are going to drop by to bring you a coffee, lunch, fresh fruit, or something they knew we liked" made it really easy for us to just go with it. They didn't ask us to make a decision, they made it for us, they had decided they were just going to decide! Sometimes it was just giving us their time. They just showed up, not expecting anything. Sometimes it was to just give a hug and try to take away the pain for even a second. It was nice when some people would come, determined to not upset us or cry, and would share funny stories or share funny things that had happened to them. Their decision took the focus away from the pain and sorrow and just gave us, for a few seconds, a break from the sadness.

A Special Evening:
One evening our daughters' boss and his wife had decided to bring us dinner. I had spoken to them the week before and honestly; I couldn't even breathe while I was talking to him. I was clearly having a very emotional day, which comes when you least expect it, and can't be

controlled.

He and his wife are fun, funny, parents that are raising teenagers. That in itself comes with great challenges but also a lot of funny stories. They had decided to bring dinner and were probably dreading this dinner. Not knowing where we would be emotionally that day; not knowing if this was going to be a sad dinner or a time when we could just share stories.

Our daughter was a shining light and was pretty funny, so in our hearts we knew they had some great stories, but you never know if you are ready to hear them. They arrived for dinner and I cannot begin to tell you how wonderful the dinner was for us. They came in probably with a mission to not make us cry or grieve more than we were but to uplift us with some humor and love. It was beautiful. They made us laugh by telling us stories, some had to do with Haley and some that were just life stories.

We shared laughter and for the first time in months, it was something that we could actually enjoy. One of our neighbors had a grand piano that they wanted to donate in Haley's name to anyone that we wanted. We of course picked the college where Haley graduated from (undergraduate and graduate) and was employed. While we had her boss in our house that evening, our neighbor wanted them to see the piano. The four of us got into the car and drove down the street to our neighbors. We went in so she could share her story and make the donation to them. As we drove back, we were literally like teenagers. We got back to our driveway, turned off the car, laughed and told stories for a half an hour. We could have gone back in the house and just visited but I remember thinking, I did this when I was a teenager. It was actually very refreshing. Them making the decision to be there was priceless. Nothing fancy, just an amazing decision and their time.

Clean

Ever have a big party? Ever have a huge party with people everywhere not knowing what to do with themselves and then have a major panic attack in the middle of it knowing you would have to clean it up. Ever have a birthday party for twenty kids and it turned out to be twenty-five? Ever feel like you just can't deal with it all?

If you've had any of this happen to you in the past you probably know that the end of the night cleanup is a nightmare. You've just dealt with a lot of people and after it's done pretty much no one ever wants to clean up the mess.

Now imagine people that are grieving. It is likely that their house will be flooded with people, there will be food, there will be people using the kitchen and restrooms, there will be people walking all over, there will be people making trash, there will be people looking for things, even if it is just a drink. To say the least it will be a tremendous ordeal. At the end of the night, or week, or month, the grieving person is left not only with their grief but with a messy house and a lot of chaos. We can tell you with utmost certainty they are not in the mood to clean it up. There will be little things like paper towels and toilet paper that will be missing. The trash will likely be full and yet there will be no end in sight to the grieving process.

If you're looking for something to do that makes a difference, here it is. Taking a moment to clean or to straighten up, take out the trash, refill the toilet paper, mop the floor, empty the trash again, sweep if possible, or do anything else that could make a difference will be a something that no one will ask you to do, but will be appreciated. Not only that, but there is also something to be said for a clean house, clean kitchen, and clean bathrooms. Even if you are like me, a clean freak, when you are going through the endless grief, you cannot even think about cleaning or honestly what your place looks like at the moment. You honestly don't really care and when someone takes it upon themselves to help with these things, it's uplifting. Depending on the people, maybe they wouldn't want you to do any more than fill the paper towels, fill the toilet paper holders, and maybe wipe down the counters. Whatever you feel they would appreciate and allow, you should do. Maybe the people grieving can't even express to you how much it would help them, or how it would make them feel. If you think you can help in this way, clean, clean. If it's your forte, do it.

It was nice:
People are in and out of the house. Food coming in and out, flowers and plants in and out, people and more people in and out. I remember seeing a friend of mine coming in the house with bags. It appeared she had gone to the grocery store to get a few things but what I found out later was that she had gone to the store, not for food that wasn't needed but to get paper plates, paper towels and low and behold toilet paper. She said to me later that all she wanted to do was do something she thought we might need done. She decided that with all the people in and out of our house that purchasing items she KNEW we would need and use, was important to her. She didn't call us to ask us what we needed, she just went and got what she knew we would need and use.

Another friend of ours sent me a message one night stating that she wanted to do something that would help us. Since we were not sending out a list of things we needed done or help with, it was up to people to figure out what would really help us on their own. Her message read "I have paid to have your house professionally cleaned for you after you take down all your Christmas decorations". I remember thinking how nice that would feel to have someone else come in and do a deep clean and all I had to do was have the house ready to be cleaned.

What she didn't know was that I was dreading taking down the Christmas decorations. That is always sad to me and it was going to be a million times harder this year. I remember telling someone before she sent me the message, I might not take down my Christmas decorations until July. I honestly didn't think I had the energy or willpower to take them down.

Knowing that someone was going to clean for me, and deep clean, once I had the decorations down, gave me motivation to take them all down, box them up, and put them away. This was something I honestly don't know how I would have mustarded the energy to do had I not had a reason to get it done. My friend wasn't cleaning my house but what she did for us was way more than having our house cleaned, it allowed us to get things done now that would have lingered for months on end.

One of our longtime friends that has been there since my husband and I got married twenty-six years ago came to our house to stay for a few weeks. She is like family, knows just about everything there is to know about my kids, our house, how we fold our towels, how I vacuum the carpet. She knows everything. I remember her doing all the laundry, putting it up, cleaning the house, taking out the trash, running to the store multiple times, and making sure the house was running as usual in the very unusual time in our life.

Going in and doing someone's laundry that you don't know, might be too much. Still, even if you can wash towels and wash cloths it may be a great way to contribute. Even running the dishwasher for someone, helps. I promise you that trying to get it together enough to even shower and gather myself each day was about all I could handle. Had it not been for people standing in the gap and getting things done, this could have been an even bigger disaster. I can't imagine the dread we would have had a month or two later when we had to take down the decorations, do all the laundry, clean the bedrooms, clean the bathrooms, clean the kitchen counters, clean the refrigerator, and clean and mop the floors. Our friends stepped up and made sure that these things were done for us. If you are thinking about what to do, examine the situation and contribute where you feel it is appropriate.

Consider Your Gift

Everyone is interested in getting something new and exciting. Well almost everyone. Finding the right gift for people is often a difficult proposition. If we had all the answers to picking the right gift, we would hand them to husbands and wives, friends and relatives, and everyone would always be happy on special occasions. We're not sure that's going to happen. Still the idea of a good gift or even the idea of an amazing gift is something that truly comes from understanding the person that you're getting the gift for at that time and the occasion that the gift will represent.

As you're considering getting a gift for someone who is in the grieving process, we would like to suggest that you also consider some additional factors that may make giving a gift more effective or at least more heartfelt. Gifts can be almost anything, but it is the strength of your friendship or relationship with someone that defines how important that gift becomes.

Strongly consider your relationship with the person and what you know about them. More to the point in doing so determine if something will be heartfelt or just another trinket or item that doesn't necessarily have the connotation you think it does. We're not saying that there is ever a bad gift, but we are strongly suggesting that sometimes choosing a better gift will be more meaningful and will help someone far more effectively. Do you really want to get something that is perishable and is gone soon or is there something you can get that will leave a lasting impression and help someone heal? Are there things that are still too difficult to see and discuss or was the loss a somewhat positive thing that allowed someone to grow?

Not all gifts have to be tangible. Some of the most important gifts can be giving of yourself, your time, and your talents. Everyone has abilities that they can share that may help during the grieving process. Your gift could be a natural ability or talent that helps out when it is needed most. Talents are given to you so that you can share them with others and perhaps the world. Some people are born to lead, some sing, some talk, some do, some are just there to comfort, some just allow others to talk while they listen. Everyone has their own gifts. During a time when the grieving are hurting it is these people with their talents that can step in and share their gifts.

As we said, the more important consideration is to determine what fits the person who is grieving. As a good friend you will be able to determine that gift that will be remembered. If you don't know, consider talking to others, or listening before you get a gift. In the end, make a decision and move forward. No matter what you choose it will help in some way.

The Gift:

Years ago, after suffering an exceedingly difficult time losing my father, I was given a solid silver cup. I never thought too much about that cup except that it represented my father's death. Well, I didn't think I did. Years passed and I kept the cup close to me from job to job as it originally was given to me from my co-workers. One day I sat down and studied it and the tender and heartfelt engraving that was put on it. It reminded me of the strength and resolution of my father and all the good things that I knew of him. I know we don't always remember people for their positives but somehow the positives from this simple gift helped me retain the positive in my life.

There is a book that I often recommend called "Hope for the Flowers". I have actually purchased this book for several people to give them insight into a different way of approaching the world. I'm sure some of them probably looked at me at first and thought I was completely insane. Here I was giving them a book about a couple of caterpillars climbing pillars of caterpillars. Thinking back on it sometimes I wonder if I was a little off in assuming that everyone could understand the intricacies of a book like this.

Looking at it now, it makes perfect sense and I'm sure that eventually it made perfect sense to them. The book is quite sensibly about growth and focuses on how we sometimes don't see all of the things around us as we are so focused on one finite goal. Years later, I had someone say something to me about that gift and make mention that it helped them see the world in a different way. I was surprised but relieved that it had gone exactly as I expected. That doesn't happen often.

I didn't give that gift to everyone. It simply didn't fit. When there were people that I knew we're driven to an excessive level I chose to give them this gift. Sometimes you need to define what more was to them. For me, when someone is grieving, I want to pick out something that helps them in some way. Not something that gets put in a drawer and never seen again but something that gives that person pause if only for a moment. Perhaps it could be a smile, perhaps it could be something else, but I always knew if I chose from the heart that I would make a difference to that person.

Friends:

There were so many things that were given to us throughout our grieving process and quite honestly are still arriving at our home months later. Each tangible gift seems to have a special meaning attached to it. The cards and letters that accompany these gifts are priceless.

Many of the gifts that arrived didn't come in a package or in the mail. They weren't dropped off or sent, they were talents. There were so many of them.

I remember a call the night of the accident. My family was in pure shock and dismay. I needed someone to talk to, to hear me yell, cry, and question everything. My youngest daughter's dance studio owner is a night owl. She and her daughter are up late every night working on the studio. I knew they would be awake, so I called them. I feel certain they could not understand a word I was saying but their compassion and support was shining through. They are very strong women and that night they were strong for me. They were not only concerned for us, but their talent was to be strong and just listen. We talked for over an hour though I don't remember what I said or if anything I said made any sense. I remember them saying "we are not letting you off the phone until someone is with you".

On their own they set up a place where people could help with monetary donations. They set goals, got it out to people all over the country and monitored it until we could take over. They also arranged a candlelight vigil at our home one evening. Our house was filled with people and as the doorbell rang, there stood an entire studio of dancers with candles just standing in silence. Though they had given more than just their time and money, they had come up with so many ways to support us, from setting up the donations to standing in our yard with so many kids. Not only were they supporting us, but they were teaching these young people how to love people that are hurting in a difficult time. All the while they were being strong for us.

Another example was a friend of ours that knows a great number of people and knows how to lead a crowd. She stepped up on day one to organize and help us wander through the weeds of the first few days. She knew all too well how to set up a ceremony since she had lost both her parents, her sister, and a few close friends. It wasn't just the setting up, it was the following through all the way until the ceremony was complete.

She made all the phone calls, asked all the right questions, followed up with us for answers, then she would make things happen. She did the behind-the-scenes things that people don't realize have to be done during these tough times. She loved our Haley and she loved us so well those few weeks following the accident and still shows her support to this day.

I can hardly believe as I look back at all the things she did, all of the decisions she made, and all the love and support she gave us without a thought.

Another friend drove four hours to get to our house to make sure that I had everything that I needed. She was very diligent and made sure I was eating, sleeping, and she was supportive at all times. She was in tune with what I needed and how I was handling my day to day.

One day she knew I needed to get out of my house, so she loaded me in the car and off we went. She allowed others to use their gifts of making things happen and she used her gift of making sure I was going to survive the days and weeks that followed. Not only did she make the drive once, she made it multiple times as the weeks went by.

Still others came to the house to help with whatever, whenever. Some close friends of ours live down the street. We had our dog and our sons' dog during that time. With people in and out of the house all day it was nerve racking for the dogs. They were confused and uptight. Our friends came up and took our dogs to their house where they stayed for two weeks while we grieved and mourned. They would sometimes bring them to see us and comfort us and then take home again. No one knows how much that helped to not have to worry about our dogs. We knew they were living the life at our neighbors and were being treated well. Their son even slept downstairs with our dogs to make sure they were ok each evening.

These are gifts that you can't put a price tag on.

There is also the gift of listening. A few weeks had passed, and I still found myself as emotional as I was the first few days. It seemed as though nothing had changed. The pain was still as heavy as it was the first day.

I called a longtime friend of mine that coached with me for years. I asked if I could come see her for a little while at her home. When I got there, I was going to discuss everyday things. It was just nice to be out of the house. I remember leaning my head back on her couch and suddenly finding myself having a full-blown emotional breakdown. She just listened. We shared tears of sorrow and I talked. She listened. Then we both cried some more. We were in this moment for hours. I remember her saying to me, "I don't think I have seen you cry for even a half second, so I knew things were really bad." I remember listening to her speak to me while I was crying right beside her.

Her gift was just listening to me. I remember her getting up from her seat and sitting beside me, not to get me to stop crying but to just listen to me more. It didn't matter what I was saying and if it made any sense, it was that she was just listening for hours.

Sometimes your gifts are not a talent people recognize as easily, maybe your talent is just listening.

Giving a gift

This particular section wasn't originally planned but it makes a lot of sense. we feel strongly that this section could easily grow if more people would come forward and point out those gifts that meant more to them. There are a significant number of gifts that are meaningful, and we hope this section can be a little help.

Gifts are something that people willingly give to someone without payment or expectations of getting anything in return. They can be a wide variety of things depending on the person giving them and the person receiving them. There is an array of things that people tend to give when someone is grieving. We have put together some of the greatest gifts we were given throughout the first few months.

Historically people have sent **sympathy cards**. This is a great way to say all the things that you want to say without getting emotional in front of those grieving. This is also good if you don't think the time is right for you to be face to face with them. I cannot begin to tell you how many cards and letters we received in our mailbox. Every single one was read when it arrived. Sometimes they were read to us, sometimes we would read them out loud, but every single card and letter was read. We have them all in a wooden box that we can read anytime we want to read them.

All these letters are filled with love. The words displayed on the card by a company, to the words handwritten. Each one has the best intentions, great love, and wonderful support behind them. We have cards in the box that actually say, "you don't know us, and we don't know you, we have just heard your story" or "we use to live in your neighborhood and our friends that still live there shared your story".

We have received letters and cards from people we have coached along the way, people we have interacted with while working out, playing tennis, working with, and doing life with each day. People sending cards and letters to people they don't even know is a beautiful testimony of loving the ones hurting no matter what and it shows sheer kindness. Our world needs more people like this in it.

Sympathy gift baskets that contain food. Giving the gift of groceries actually can help those grieving. Sending a few premade meals is a great way to show love and it allows them to have something in the freezer after the meal train has stopped. Sending a Door Dash or Grub Hub certificate allows them to order a meal from a delivery service, which can be nice once the meal train is complete.

I remember going to the porch one morning after getting a message from a friend that works with me. Her comment was "I bought you some breakfast food and put it in the cooler on the porch" I remember another co-worker sending us a message that the pizza was on its way to our house. It was a nice treat for the kids and a great way to just show love and support.

A friend of ours, whom I coached her daughter, had heard through the grapevine that I wasn't eating much but what I was eating was fruit. She and her daughters brought a container of fruit more than one time to me. One of those days was Christmas morning. They were filling the cooler on the porch with breakfast food on Christmas morning, one container was filled with diced fruit. I knew that container was for me.

We received **dinners** that were absolutely delicious, and it was nice to have them brought to the house. We could then thank the providers. Sometimes it was sent to us through a gift card in a premade box which was equally as nice.

As you go through the grieving process, you just wonder how in the world can you thank all these people that have done so much for you. When someone actually walked in the house sometimes there were tears and sometimes it was just a nice hug accompanied by a nice dinner. It's always nice to say thank you in person.

Multiple people brought **lunch** to the house during the weeks following the service. It was nice when they didn't ask if they could, they just said, "we are bringing you lunch" or they just showed up and dropped off lunch.   Asking people what they need or want, is sometimes overwhelming and the usually answer will be "nothing". Sometimes they do tell you, you just need to make sure you are listening. My husband and I both have been in sales most of our adult lives and the number one thing you do in sales is "listen". This is what you should do with those who are grieving. They will tell you what they need how they can, and it is important for you to hear them.

One night I remember sitting in my kitchen with a few friends around the table just listening to conversations going on throughout the house. Someone mentioned **pizza** and I remember saying "Pizza sound so good" and before I could think about anything else, they were on the phone ordering pizza. They were listening for signs of things we needed or things that we might want at the time. They didn't ask if I wanted pizza, they just listened to what I said, they knew I personally had not been eating much, and they ordered it. I was getting pizza that evening whether I wanted to eat pizza or not, and to be honest, it tasted delicious.

Meal Prep is something that many people do now to make their life a little easier throughout the year. Some people are really good at it and some people lack the confidence, patience, and time it requires. If this is something that you love to do, do it for those that are grieving. Prepping meals for them to take out of the freezer or refrigerator when there is no longer a meal train can allow them to cook but not be overwhelmed with all the details of grocery shopping, prepping the food, and preparing it. It makes life just a little easier for them during this time. It also shows off your meal prep skills!

I remember a friend of ours that is a trainer also does meal prep and life coaching. She contacted me to let me know she was coming to town and wanted to spend a little time with me. Knowing that we were going to share some tears, memories, and stories, could have been overwhelming, but I agreed. When I told her we should meet she said "would you like to meal prep together". To me that was a great way for us to spend time in a positive way and also have a task on hand to focus on while visiting. We shared a few tears when she arrived and then we got right into the kitchen to start prepping. It was so nice to have something to focus on while just sharing stories and time together. If you are one that is good at meal prepping, I highly recommend you share your talents while visiting. I can't imagine that most people wouldn't love this. Of course, doing this when the time is right is key. Our time together was after the meal train had ended and things had started to quiet down around our home. It was perfect.

A weighted blanket or a soft and comfy blanket is a wonderful gift. Those that are grieving can sometimes suffer from insomnia and may have trouble falling asleep. They may be able to go to sleep from exhaustion but not stay asleep. A weighted blanket has been proven to help with anxiety and feel like a hug. This can absolutely calm you and be what you need during the evening hours.

A few weeks after the accident my husband knew that we were not sleeping well and sometimes not at all. He purchased a weighted blanket for me. I had never had one, nor really asked for one, but studies show that it helps with anxiety and sleepless nights. I would have to agree there is a certain amount of comfort that is given with a weighted blanket. It really does give you a sense of a hug and seems to help.

A comfy blanket is one that can bring you exactly what it was made for, comfort. When people are grieving, they need to be warm and comfortable, and this blanket will do both. I have never been a great sleeper and after the accident, I didn't want to sleep at all. Sleeping was so hard for me because I knew when I woke up, I would have the same reality. Every day started like that for me, so I never really wanted to go to sleep. Maybe it was that I didn't want to wake up to the reality.

It was a week or so after the service that a friend of mine and her daughter came by the house and left a package on the porch. They sent me a message to let me know they had left the package. I went to get it and inside I found **a very comfy blanket** that was just beautiful, warm, and so comforting. It was just what I needed at the time. I spent a lot of time in a chair or on the couch by the fireplace just trying to get two thoughts together. Wrapping up with this blanket was perfect.

My aunt sent me a book and a very comfy blanket that I could travel with from room to room or even take with me when in the car. Many of my youngest daughters' friends brought her comfy slippers and blankets, things that made her feel cozy and comfortable. There is a sense of comfort when you are wrapped in a nice blanket. It's what comfort food does for you, just in a different way.

Sending a **good book** might be a great way to allow them to remove themselves from their grief for even a small moment and allow their minds to have a break for a little while. If they are not a reader, maybe sending them an easy read or a video to watch would be better. We received a lot of books during this time. Many were books about grieving, being parents and grieving, and more. There were many and were giving that will take some time to read. Maybe it is too soon to read, but in time will help in the healing process. There were many self-help and healing books however one book my aunt sent me was an easy lighthearted read full of illustrations about friendship. Friends helping friends. It's a great one that I will want to go back and enjoy for years to come and share with other people. If you have a good book, doesn't need to be heavy in content, just something to allow those grieving to preoccupy their mind for a short time, it a great gift.

Plants and Flowers. Sending plants is a great way to allow the grieving to have something they can enjoy for a long time. You can put them in colorful pots so that everything doesn't seem gloomy. Finding the right plant is key, maybe one that doesn't require a lot of care would be ideal.

Sending flowers is something we talked about in a previous chapter. We suggest if you are going to send them pick colorful ones. Colorful flowers that look and seem happy might be the best option. Remember that waiting to send them when the grieving family is once again alone may be the best decision. They may need a pick-me-up and colorful flowers might just be the key they need for a smile that day.

One of the bouquets that stood out the most was a large bouquet of multi-colored flowers, some large and some small with very vibrant colors sent from my daughters' employer. They were not only beautiful in color, but it was also in a nice arrangement. They were what our daughter would have wanted. They were like her personality, colorful and bright. They also came when we didn't have any other flowers in the house, so they were refreshing.

Send a **Seed packet with Forget-me-not seeds** or wildflowers. There are so many companies that make packets that you just plant the packet, and the flowers grow. Not a lot of work, just a simple plant in the ground. A few people gave us the seed packets that will be planted in months to come. I feel certain that when we look at those flowers blooming it will bring us a bit of happiness.

Jewelry is a great way to give a gift that they can have for a lifetime. It helps them keep their loved one close to them. Jewelry is a great way to share a certain saying or a person's name or birthstone. There are so many companies that put out beautiful jewelry that don't break the bank.

I received a package one morning from a very dear friend who had coached with me early in my career. As I opened the box, I found a necklace with my daughter's name on it. It was beautiful and I wear it all the time. I had another friend whose daughter went and purchased a necklace for my daughter with her initial on it. Shortly after that, I received the same type of necklace from her mom, in the mail. I also received two different necklaces that had angel wings on them. They were beautiful.

One day I received a message that someone had left something on my porch. I went to retrieve it and found two boxes, one for my youngest daughter and one for me. Inside we found bracelets with words of encouragement on them. The gifts were simply perfect and again something we wear and think of those that gave them and our sweet daughter/sister always. I alternate wearing all these things and love them all equally. There is so much beauty in the concept of sending jewelry.

A garden stone or statue. Giving these so that they can put them in their flower garden or in the garden is a great way for them to remember their loved one when they are outside. There are so many of these to choose from but all of them bring great joy to those grieving. A group of friends that I play tennis with and have known for a long time came by the house one day to give us a Garden Angel. It is a beautiful garden statue of an angel. We will place this in our flower garden this spring and I will always be reminded of their friendships and it is yet another thing to remind me of Haley. People can really appreciate these things for many years to come.

A scripture cards and words of encouragement. These gifts come on a stand and you can change them out each day or each week. They are great to have near an area you most frequently visit. They are all different and come with holders that can be easily set on your desk, on the kitchen windowsill, or on an end table or bed side table. They are words of encouragement and it's something that grieving people need daily.

A **Custom painting or photo** of their loved ones is a great way to share something special with them. You can also illustrate them on the computer and make a painting, watercolor, or pencil art with a photo that is nice to give to the family.

It was about a week after the ceremony. I had gone to see my niece and nephew and get away from the four walls I was living in. When I returned home that evening, there was a large box in my back seat. My nephew had ordered a beautiful picture of my daughter on canvas. The canvas read "I never left you...." and had many amazing words follow. At first, I was worried about opening it and having the heartache of seeing something I had not read or seen before. The day I actually opened it was a day I needed that encouragement, that saying, and that picture more than ever. I was struggling with missing Haley so much. I opened it to find the words written just for me, that day, at that moment. It was exactly what I needed. It now hangs in my office for me to see and I am reminded of what a beautiful gift.

One of my daughter's dear friends sent us a painting that she had illustrated on the computer and ordered online. It was such a beautiful gift that truly reminded me of how much these people loved her and how much we loved her too. It was just breathtaking, a picture of her in a unique way made with tons of love. It now is displayed in our living room for all to appreciate.

The seniors that were coached by Haley and I had a canvas made of a picture of Haley on it. Beautifully illustrated and colored with a beautiful bible verse. It too will hang in our home and remind us of what an impact she made on so many.

A picture of their loved one is a beautiful gift for those that are grieving. Though depending on the timing, it is given, it may take them a little time to open and appreciate the beauty of it, it's a nice gift.

A **nice porcelain dish** or an **engraved piece** that the loved one can use each day or have in a special place as a remind of their loved one. There are many choices that can be personalized with a message that means a lot to both you and those grieving.

A **small box** they can save flower petals and other remembrances is a wonderful gift. We all received these types of gifts. They are displayed or used all over our home. Each time we see them or use them, it is a way for us to remember that people are thinking and praying for us daily.

Candles are such a nice gift. When things seem so solemn and gray, it is nice for the people grieving to light a candle that will send a beautiful fragrance throughout the room as well as share a very peaceful light. I received candles from friends and family that smell wonderful and truly bring calm to a very chaotic atmosphere. The grief is certainly so heavy and lighting that candle and just watching the flame flicker is very calming. Maybe you meditate and having a fragrance and small light will help you calm your inner being.

A smoothing stone or a handheld cross to cling to perfectly. These are things people can put in their purse or pocket and have with them at all times. It shows them that you understand they are grieving, and it reminds them that people understand how much grief you are facing. They might not know the exact pain, but it is them acknowledging that they know you are grieving. They can hold onto the cross or rub the stone as a reminder that these difficult times are real and should be dealt with one minute at a time.

I received a cross that I keep in my purse. It fits perfectly in my hand and it has a small story about the cross with it. I have talked to other moms that have walked this same journey, and they often have something like this with them.

The smoothing stone is a round, smooth piece that many men and women can have in their pocket. It is something you can hold onto or rub that reminds you to just take one minute at a time, one day at a time. There is something comforting about having one of these. One of my co-workers gave me one that had an angel on the top. I always keep that in my purse. It reminds me that she knows I am grieving, and it also gives me something to hold on to when I need to be reminded that people are praying or thinking of us.

A suncatcher or Light Catcher is a small stained-glass piece designed to be hung near a light source (usually in a window). Most of them are a decorative piece, some hang from a ribbon or string, others have a suction cup on the back that allows them to hang from the window. On a sunny day, with just the right angle, the sun shines on them, dispersing the light and colors. It catches the sunlight and usually shines a beautiful rainbow of color in your room. It can also be in just a few colors, maybe the loved one's favorite color, so when the sun hits it they see that color and are reminded of their loved one. Suncatchers come in all shapes and sizes.

We have always told our kids that **rainbows** mean "everything is going to be ok". It was a story that we developed when I was pregnant with Haley. We have shared that story with all our kids but always shared the first time we said that after seeing a rainbow over the fields near our home.

Though we know that the actual rainbow doesn't make everything ok, it does give some people a ray of hope. There are many myths among many different cultures around the world containing the rainbow. Some see it as a symbol of a "bridge" for gods to cross from earth. The ancient Japanese believed that the rainbow allowed their deceased ancestors to return to earth using the bridge. The Navajo Indians believed that it was the path (bridge) to the holy spirits. There was even a legend that is often told to kids and that there is a pot of gold buried at the end of the rainbow that a leprechaun placed and watches over. There are many ways that rainbows are the symbol of hope in many cultures. In the Bible when Noah was on the ark with his family and all the animals it was raining for forty days and forty nights. The earth was fully flooded. This story began in Genesis 6:9.

After the rain stopped a rainbow appeared in the sky to symbolize the covenant between all life on earth and God and a promise that no flood would happen again. The Bible is very clear about what the rainbow symbolizes.

There is something about people seeing a rainbow that gives them hope. Whether it is in the sky or is displayed by a suncatcher, it has a little peace that comes along with it. I personally use it as my sign of hope. I have a few suncatchers that were given to us and they are hanging in different windows of our home. It makes my heart happy when I see a rainbow coming from the sun catcher. Some days they just show up on my walls or floor and I am constantly reminded of the hope that I have and how beautiful the rainbow is to me.

A windchime or windcatcher is a great gift. It is another way to give us a beautiful sight or maybe music to our ears. The wind hits this type of percussion instruments constructed from suspended rods, bells, tubes and other objects that are often made of tin, steel, or hard plastic. When the wind hits them, they make a very distinct sound and pitch. It's like a simple song that you have never heard before that brings you a sense of peace. Many will say that wind chimes attract positive energy and that is why they are given to people that are grieving. The gentle sounds of tinkling emanate from the windchime which helps positive energy linger in the space it is hung. Many people place them outside so when the wind blows, the chimes touch one another and make the beautiful sound of nature's music. This can remind them of the beauty of their loved one. They can also be moved inside and hung by a window so when the window is open and the air enters, the chimes will be heard. We were given a few sets of windchimes and will hang these outside so that we can hear their beautiful music. They are not only beautiful to see but even more beautiful to hear.

A windcatcher is a piece of art that moves with the wind and adds beauty to an area. Some windcatchers are like pinwheels while others are complex pieces of art that move randomly in the wind. Like windchimes these are a fantastic gift to remember someone by.

An Angel is a gift to remind the grieving of their loved one. It also is a way to give them hope that we have angels watching over us. Many people send Angels when someone has lost a loved one. Angels where something that became very prevalent after our daughter's accident. People were writing letters and messages stating what an angel she was and then people started sending angels to us. To be honest, the first few days were hard to accept anything. As sweet as the angels were, we really just wanted our sweet daughter back. A long-time neighbor had been coming to the house to help with many things. While we were making plans for the Celebration of Life, she approached us about purchasing Christmas trees for us to have at the ceremony (it was in December) and having people bring Angel ornaments to fill the trees. It was a way to allow people to do something special and unique. People were eager to help, and she knew this would be beautiful. We loved the idea, and the message went out.

During the ceremony there were hundreds of people and the trees began to fill up with angels. The Angels were of all sizes and shapes. There were Angels holding flowers, Angels with Bible verses, Angels with little animals and birds, and they were all were precious and beautiful. Those trees were filled, every branch, every area on the tree was filled. It was a beautiful sight to see in the large sanctuary. Nine-foot-tall forest green Christmas trees that were all lit up with brilliant white lights covered with amazing and wonderful angels.

I remember after the ceremony going over to the trees and seeing hundreds of angels hanging on the tree's branches. Some had names on them, some were handmade, some resembled our sweet daughter, some had one of her favorite items included. There was one that had a diet coke, which was Haley's favorite drink.

As people left the church our friends began to box all the angels up so that they could take down the trees. They had not planned to keep them boxed up. The next day they arrived at our home, which is filled with Christmas decorations already, and began to put these two trees back up except this time it was in our home. This was for us to enjoy for the days that followed and every single Christmas from here on out. It was an amazing idea that will continue to bring us great joy for years to come. Knowing that we can put these Christmas trees back up and see all the angels that represent the people that loved us so well during this time in our life will be amazing. We have since been sent more and more angels that are accompanied by letters from people far and wide. They will be added to our angel trees next year.

Parting Thoughts

Right now, you're probably reeling with all the thoughts that have been thrown at you during the last few pages. Maybe you're reeling with all the thoughts we've thrown at you in the past 100 pages but still it's a lot to digest. Suffice it to say that as people we have to react to a significant number of different stimuli every day. People who are going through the grieving process have to react to more. Well, maybe not more, but at least they have to react to more prevalent stimuli. There just is no escape from it.

With that in mind we strongly recommend that you take some time and consider people going through the grieving process as temporarily mentally off limits or at least temporarily mentally compromised. This does not mean that they are any less intelligent or that they are in any way crazy but instead means that they will process data much differently than you will for a while. As you are communicating with them you have to consider that their mind is constantly being affected and over stimulated by memories and emotions that you may not be privy to or have not experienced at all.

Watch closely, remember that sometimes people need help. Be that help when you can but let them get help if they need it. Getting professional help when you are grieving is not something to be ashamed of, it is something that may need to be done. If you are asked for a name of someone to help, assist in any way you can. It is up to you, well, all of us, to be there for anyone who is going through the grieving process. They say it takes a village to raise a child, but we feel it may take a village to grieve well. There will be a lot going on, and yes, that is said too much, but it is true.

Take a deep breath and listen. Yeah, we know, we've said that multiple times during this book. It is in fact probably at the core of just about everything you should do. When you are dealing with anyone involved in a complex situation listening is far more important than interjecting. You really need to take that step back and be aware of how they're processing data right now. This will be a journey and if you had the slightest inclination to read this book you have taken a step towards helping others. There is no fixing grief easily. There is no making it better by words and even potentially by actions.

With that being said it is always possible your kind words will make a difference and even more possible that your presence will be comforting and make a difference as well. There is no way we can stress enough how difficult grief is on a person. There are a host of studies on the effects of grief on the human body and how devastating it can be. As you consider your words and actions remember this is a real event and having real consequences on the person who is grieving. Be patient, be kind, be loving, but mostly be there.

We know this will be tough, but we believe in everyone and know that there are many strong people in the world willing to make a difference. Thank you for being one of those people. Thank you for putting up with our stories and suggestions and thank you for caring enough to try to be there for someone who is grieving.

Appendix:

The Not to Say and Do checklist.

1. What happened – Don't ask them what happened, if they want to tell you they will, but don't ask. Do your own research if you need to know.
2. He or She is in a better place – Let them determine if they want to think this or not, sharing that with them doesn't usually help those grieving.
3. God needed her more – Those who are grieving are often missing the person they lost more than can be imagined. This lays blame on God, and at the same time may minimize the feelings of the grieving.
4. God knew – God knew when he put, he or she on earth, when he was going to take them. Not something you need to reference at this time, it usually doesn't help the grieving.
5. You and your spouse will need counseling – Yes most will need counseling but telling them this now doesn't help.
6. God never gives you more than you can handle. This doesn't help because many people grieving is already beyond what they can handle. Once again it may put blame on God as well. Consider your words carefully when thinking about this type of statement.
7. Just push through it – This seems pushy and isn't want a grieving person needs, they need compassion and support not direction.
8. Don't Cry- Let them cry, cry with them, crying is good for anyone that is grieving. Crying is good for you as well.
9. Death comes in Threes – This should NEVER be said to a grieving person. It is not true or at least not provable and doesn't help at all!
10. I know how you feel – Unless you have lived the exact same life as the grieving and you have had the exact same thing happen in your life, you don't know exactly how they feel, don't compare. Instead consider words like "I can only imagine" or similar to let them explain their feelings.

11. Are you ok or how are you doing – Neither of these need to be asked to a grieving person. They are not ok, they are grieving. How are they doing, Well, they are grieving, so probably not very well.

12. You are strong – Maybe the person is normally strong or appears to be strong, but when you are grieving you don't feel strong, and you don't want to be strong. You want the ability to be weak, vulnerable, and be where you need to be at the time. Strong puts pressure on them.

13. You'll find a way – Yes, they will find a way, but this approach sounds pushy and not appropriate for those that are hurting and grieving. It puts more pressure on them, and trust us, they are feeling enough pressure.

14. If they could be here, they would be – Yes, if they could be they would be, but this may create additional helplessness depending on the situation. Set it aside and listen and know that for many people it is difficult to let go. Don't add to the divide.

15. This is your new reality – No one needs to be reminded that their reality has all changed, and they now are going to have to begin a new reality. Don't remind them, they already know.

The to Do and Say Checklist

1. A Meal Train. thinking ahead may be a gift that keeps on giving to someone who is grieving. This is a super idea every time.
2. Recipe cards: if you are considering giving food remember that during this time many people get more food gifts than anything else. If your dish is especially unique, consider including a recipe card as a special gift so the person can enjoy your culinary masterpiece over and over again.
3. Be There: that is the best place to be and being there makes a statement that you are looking out for their best interests.
4. Send texts and emails: even if you can't be there making those simple statements in a text or email will allow a family or person to read at their leisure and respond when they can. Remember they may not have their phone or even have their phone on during this time so be patient for the reply.
5. Help: if you don't know what to do find some way to help. It seems like an easy statement, but the simplest things become overlooked in the pure chaos of a loss. Something as easy as emptying the trash could change the world for the people involved.
6. I don't know how you feel: acknowledging that you are not a definitive source of how a person is feeling during the grieving process may well allow you to communicate more effectively and may encourage the person grieving to reach out to you.
7. Cry together: sometimes that's all it takes. Sometimes you don't need to talk or do anything except cry with the grieving. After all you may be grieving too.
8. Make Decisions: there is a lot going on. If you are a self-starter or understand what needs to be done take small decisions and move forward. Don't push too hard but listen and know what needs to be done. Then make it happen.
9. Clean: you know things will get dirty with a lot of people around. Even if it's not noticed you will feel good about cleaning a little

and helping out.

10. Consider your gift: remember the gift is something special if chosen right can last forever. Consider your gift and consider who you're giving it to before you buy.

About the Authors

Andrew and Pamela

Pamela was born in a small town in Indiana, where she was placed up for adoption at an early age and adopted by a family of three. At that moment she gained not only a mom and a dad but a big brother, her rock, her supporter, the one that forever stands by her side, her only sibling. Pamela went to middle school and high school in Lexington Kentucky and received her bachelor's degree from Eastern Kentucky University. As of 2021, she has been married to husband, Stacy, for 26 years and they have three beautiful children, Haley (25), Hayden (21) and Hadley (15). Pam's love for helping others began at a young age where she found her way while coaching. She spent 10 years coaching Division 1A cheerleading at the prestigious, Vanderbilt University and then an additional two years at the Lipscomb University. While coaching she also was in sales where she loved helping customers find their exact needs. She has always had a passion to not only help others but to write. This book allowed her to do both. This is her first book published. When she has spare time, she enjoys her family that keeps her grounded, any outdoor activities, the beach, reading, and a little bit of shopping.

Andrew was born in the same small town in Indiana about five years before Pam. He still remembers to this day the first day that he met his little sister and played and took care of her from an incredibly early age. Until the age of 15 the family moved at least once per year and finally settled in Lexington Ky. Andrew spent a significant amount of time reading and writing short stories and poetry from an incredibly early age. He published his first book, "A Slice of Passion", in 2005. It was a book of poetry that had been compiled from dozens of years of work. In 2015 he published "The Theft and other Short Stories" After he was challenged to self-publish a book. In 2016 he published his first novel "Vengeful Son" and began building a franchise with that book. The Masterson Files (The series containing "Vengeful Son") Now contains 5 books and has 12 in outline form. Andrew's work as a quality engineer and system architect also gave him credit for a series of instructional books for site relationship management systems and a variety of quality documents and development lifecycles. In Andrew's spare time he has a passion for a considerable number of hobbies and his family which he considers paramount.

The Haley Sue Foundation

Out of everything there can still be a positive no matter how negative that thing may be. In 2020 Haley Sue Pearson was a vibrant and alive teacher, singer, friend, coach, wife, daughter, niece, cousin, and was working towards changing the world. She wasn't necessarily changing the world by some grandiose gesture but instead she was doing it in an intelligent and concise manner, one person at a time.

Her patient way and adaptable mindset made her everyone's best friend. Some people would say the very idea of her being everyone's best friend was difficult, but Haley honestly was everyone's best friend. She listened and more important she heard. She wanted to consistently make a difference with every person she came in contact with. She was not in any way shallow or fake but instead was highly adaptable and quickly understood the needs of others.

As a teacher Haley found the lowest common denominator quickly and showed others what was necessary to succeed. As a friend Haley paid attention to who you were and made you the center of her universe. In each thing Haley did she pushed for excellence and she pressed to be the best that she could be.

It is with that thought of excellence and achievement and willingness to sacrifice to change the world even a little that the Haley Sue Foundation was built upon. Each year the Haley Sue foundation will make a difference in a young person's life by giving a scholarship to help in college. The foundation will also be involved in changing the world every day. Whether it is small gesture or a massive movement the foundation will inspire the passions of both young and old and keep shining the light of Haley Sue. If you believe that everyone who wants to make a difference deserves a chance, then please visit thehaleysuefoundation.org and consider helping to change the world one person at a time.

CPSIA information can be obtained
at www.ICGtesting.com
Printed in the USA
JSHW031008040621
15466JS00006B/77